THE SENATORS

Fenn Publishing Company Ltd.

THE SENATORS:
Celebrating Ottawa's Quest for Lord Stanley's Cup

A Fenn Publishing Book / First Published in 2007

All rights reserved
Copyright 2007 © Moydart Press
No part of this book may be reproduced or transmitted in any form, or by any means, electronic or mechanical, including photocopying, recording, or by any information storage and retrieval system, without the written permission of the publisher.

The content, opinion and subject matter contained herein is the written expression of the author and does not reflect the opinion or ideology of the publisher, or that of the publisher's representatives.

Designed by First Image

Fenn Publishing Company Ltd.
Bolton, Ontario, Canada
Printed in Canada

The publisher gratefully acknowledges the support of the Canada Council for the Arts and the Ontario Arts Council for its publishing program. We acknowledge the support of the Government of Ontario through the Ontario Media Development Corporation's Ontario Book Initiative.

We acknowledge the financial support of the Government of Canada through the Book Publishing Industry Development Program (BPIDP) for our publishing activities.

Care has been taken to trace ownership of copyright material in this book and to secure permissions. The publishers will gladly receive any information that will enable them to rectify errors or omissions.

Acknowledgements
The author would like to thank the few but important people who have made this book possible. First, to publisher Jordan Fenn for his ongoing support of these books. Next, to the excellent design team of Michael Gray and Rob Scanlan at First Image. Also to Katie Hunt-Morr at Reuters and Steve Poirier at the Hockey Hall of Fame in Toronto. Lastly, to Emma Grace for her support. Without help in one form or another from the above people, the book could not have happened.

Photo Credits
All photos courtesy of Reuters except—p. 9 (Hockey Hall of Fame), p. 102 (City of Ottawa archives), p. 103 & 104 (Hockey Hall of Fame archives), p. 107 (National Archives)

///////// 2006–2007 Regular Season & Playoffs in Review \\\\\\\\\

THE SENATORS

Celebrating Ottawa's Quest for Lord Stanley's Cup

Andrew Podnieks

Fenn Publishing Company Ltd.
Bolton, Canada

Contents

Organization 8
Birth of the Ottawa Senators 9
Training Camp Roster 10

The Regular Season, 2006–07

October 4, 2006	Ottawa 4 at Toronto 1	12
October 5, 2006	Toronto 6 at Ottawa 0	12
October 7, 2006	Buffalo 4 at Ottawa 3	13
October 12, 2006	Calgary 1 at Ottawa 0	13
October 14, 2006	Ottawa 3 at Montreal 2	14
October 19, 2006	Colorado 2 at Ottawa 1	14
October 21, 2006	New Jersey 1 at Ottawa 8	15
October 24, 2006	Ottawa 6 at Toronto 2	15
October 26, 2006	Toronto 2 at Ottawa 7	16
October 28, 2006	Ottawa 1 at Boston 2	16
October 31, 2006	Ottawa 2 at Montreal 4	16
November 4, 2006	Carolina 3 at Ottawa 2	17
November 6, 2006	Ottawa 3 at Washington 4 (OT)	18
November 8, 2006	Ottawa 4 at Atlanta 5	18
November 10, 2006	Ottawa 6 at Pittsburgh 3	18
November 11, 2006	Ottawa 3 at Boston 4	19
November 13, 2006	Montreal 6 at Ottawa 3	20
November 15, 2006	Ottawa 4 at Buffalo 2	20
November 17, 2006	Ottawa 2 at New Jersey 3	21
November 18, 2006	Buffalo 1 at Ottawa 4	21
November 20, 2006	Minnesota 3 at Ottawa 5	22
November 22, 2006	Ottawa 3 at Philadelphia 2	22
November 24, 2006	Ottawa 6 at Florida 4	23
November 26, 2006	Ottawa 1 at Tampa Bay 3	23
November 28, 2006	Ottawa 4 at Carolina 1	24
November 30, 2006	Florida 0 at Ottawa 6	24
December 2, 2006	Tampa Bay 2 at Ottawa 5	25
December 5, 2006	Ottawa 4 at NY Islanders 2	25
December 6, 2006	Ottawa 2 at Washington 6	26
December 9, 2006	NY Rangers 3 at Ottawa 1	26
December 10, 2006	Ottawa 2 at Columbus 6	27
December 12, 2006	Ottawa 3 at Detroit 2	27
December 14, 2006	Ottawa 0 at Nashville 6	28
December 16, 2006	Ottawa 3 at Buffalo 1	28
December 19, 2006	Boston 7 at Ottawa 2	28
December 21, 2006	Tampa Bay 4 at Ottawa 2	29
December 23, 2006	Ottawa 6 at Philadelphia 3	30
December 27, 2006	NY Islanders 0 at Ottawa 2	30
December 29, 2006	NY Rangers 0 at Ottawa 1	31
December 30, 2006	Ottawa 3 at Toronto 2	31
January 1, 2007	Atlanta 3 at Ottawa 2	32
January 3, 2007	Buffalo 3 at Ottawa 6	32
January 6, 2007	New Jersey 3 at Ottawa 2	32
January 7, 2007	Philadelphia 1 at Ottawa 6	33
January 9, 2007	Boston 2 at Ottawa 5	34
January 11, 2007	Ottawa 6 at NY Rangers 4	34
January 13, 2007	Montreal 3 at Ottawa 8	35
January 16, 2007	Washington 2 at Ottawa 5	35
January 18, 2007	Vancouver 2 at Ottawa 1	36
January 20, 2007	Ottawa 3 at Boston 0	36

2007 All-Star Game 37

January 27, 2007	Boston 1 at Ottawa 3	38
January 29, 2007	Ottawa 1 at Montreal 3	38
January 30, 2007	Washington 2 at Ottawa 3	39
February 3, 2007	Toronto 3 at Ottawa 2	39
February 7, 2007	Ottawa 2 at Buffalo 3	40
February 8, 2007	Montreal 1 at Ottawa 4	40
February 10, 2007	Ottawa 5 at Montreal 3	41
February 14, 2007	Florida 0 at Ottawa 4	41
February 17, 2007	Atlanta 3 at Ottawa 5	42
February 20, 2007	Edmonton 3 at Ottawa 4	42
February 22, 2007	Ottawa 5 at Buffalo 6	43
February 24, 2007	Buffalo 5 at Ottawa 6	43
February 27, 2007	Ottawa 4 at Carolina 2	44
February 28, 2007	Carolina 0 at Ottawa 2	44
March 2, 2007	Ottawa 2 at Atlanta 4	45
March 4, 2007	Ottawa 3 at Chicago 4	45
March 6, 2007	Pittsburgh 5 at Ottawa 4	46
March 8, 2007	Toronto 1 at Ottawa 5	46
March 10, 2007	Ottawa 3 at Toronto 4	47
March 13, 2007	Ottawa 3 at NY Rangers 2	47
March 15, 2007	NY Islanders 2 at Ottawa 5	48
March 17, 2007	Philadelphia 2 at Ottawa 3	48
March 18, 2007	Ottawa 3 at Pittsburgh 4	48
March 20, 2007	Ottawa 4 at St. Louis 2	49
March 22, 2007	Ottawa 4 at Florida 2	50
March 24, 2007	Ottawa 7 at Tampa Bay 2	50
March 27, 2007	Boston 3 at Ottawa 2	50
March 30, 2007	Montreal 2 at Ottawa 5	51
March 31, 2007	Ottawa 5 at NY Islanders 2	52
April 3, 2007	Ottawa 1 at New Jersey 2	52
April 5, 2007	Pittsburgh 3 at Ottawa 2	53
April 7, 2007	Ottawa 6 at Boston 3	53

The Players 54
Final Statistics, 2007 Playoffs 56
Final NHL Standings 56
2007 NHL Playoff Results 57

Eastern Conference Quarter-finals:
Pittsburgh Penguins vs. Ottawa Senators

April 11, 2007	Pittsburgh 3 at Ottawa 6	58
April 14, 2007	Pittsburgh 4 at Ottawa 3	60
April 15, 2007	Ottawa 4 at Pittsburgh 2	62
April 17, 2007	Ottawa 2 at Pittsburgh 1	64
April 19, 2007	Pittsburgh 0 at Ottawa 3	66

Eastern Conference Semi-finals:
Ottawa Senators vs. New Jersey Devils

April 26, 2007	Ottawa 5 at New Jersey 4	68
April 28, 2007	Ottawa 2 at New Jersey 3	70
April 30, 2007	New Jersey 0 at Ottawa 2	72
May 2, 2007	New Jersey 2 at Ottawa 3	74
May 5, 2007	Ottawa 3 at New Jersey 2	76

Eastern Conference Finals:
Ottawa Senators vs. Bufalo Sabres

May 10, 2007	Ottawa 5 at Buffalo 2	78
May 12, 2007	Ottawa 4 at Buffalo 3	80
May 14, 2007	Buffalo 0 at Ottawa 1	82
May 16, 2007	Buffalo 3 at Ottawa 2	84
May 19, 2007	Ottawa 3 at Buffalo 2	86

Stanley Cup Finals:
Ottawa Senators vs. Anaheim Ducks

May 28, 2007	Ottawa 2 at Anaheim 3	88
May 30, 2007	Ottawa 0 at Anaheim 1	90
June 2, 2007	Anaheim 3 at Ottawa 5	92
June 4, 2007	Anaheim 3 at Ottawa 2	94
June 6, 2007	Ottawa 2 at Anaheim 6	96

Previous Appearances in the Playoffs, 1918-34	98
Previous Appearances in the Playoffs, 1992-2006	99
All-Time Playoff Record	100
All-Time Draft Choices	101
Ottawa Silver Seven	102
The Original Senators	103
Tribute to Frank Finnigan	104
The Modern Senators	105
Birth of the Stanley Cup	106
Photo Gallery	108

Chris Phillips and Sidney Crosby collide along the boards.

New Jersey's David Clarkson goes for a spill as Anton Volchenkov clears the puck.

Introduction

When the various members of the Ottawa Senators gathered for the start of training camp back in September 2006, no one was quiet sure what the team consisted of or was capable of producing over the course of a grueling season. Yes, the Sens had plenty of talent, and they had a good mix of youth and experience, but goaltending was a problem and so was playoff under-achieving. There was also the significant matter of developing into a team and being ready to go deep into the playoffs.

More than 100 games later, a season of unequivocal success has allayed many of the fears and worries of fans and management. This Senators team produced the most vivid hockey memories for the city in 80 years, fighting into the Stanley Cup finals before succumbing to Anaheim in five games. The road from training camp to Cup finals, however, was hardly smooth.

The first game of the season was a convincing 4-1 win over the hated Leafs right at Air Canada Centre. It was a great start, however, that was forgotten less than 24 hours later when those same Leafs hammered the Sens 6-0 at Scotiabank Place. Those two games represented a microcosm of the first part of Ottawa's year—one night, the team looked like world-beaters; the next, like also-rans. It seemed that for every game the team scored and played well it answered with a lethargic game in which its opponent out-hustled and outplayed the Sens.

Something happened over Christmas, though. The Senators came back after the holiday break and shut out the Islanders and Rangers in consecutive home games, 2-0 and 1-0, and from these results they gained confidence and momentum. Over the next eleven games, they built a 9-2 record and developed into one of the top scoring teams in the league. Everything was going as planned. Dany Heatley, on his way to a second straight 50-goal season, was the finisher, while linemate Jason Spezza became a dominant offensive player in the league. The third member of that line, Daniel Alfredsson, added another potent dimension.

At the same time, the role players contributed enormously to the team's success. Chris Neil played with a physical edge without losing control or focus and chipping in with timely goals and big hits. Mike Fisher was a tenacious two-way forward, and the defence was simply impenetrable. Wade Redden and Chris Phillips led the way, but Andrej Meszaros was the leading shot-blocker in the game and a rock solid inside his own blueline.

In early January, during the team's first hot streak, the Sens made a high-impact deal by acquiring Mike Comrie from Phoenix. Not a big player, he was another skilled forward with a golden touch around the net and good skating legs. Soon after the All-Star break, the team went on another tear, winning eight of nine games in the latter part of February.

As the team's skaters developed a cohesion, its goaltending was also sorting itself out, and this meant Ray Emery establishing himself as the number-one man and Martin Gerber as his backup. Emery was playing with a maturity and poise that was, quite simply, unexpected, and the more he played, the better he played. By the time the playoffs arrived, the Senators were a team with all elements firing on all cylinders.

But the playoffs had long been a psychological barrier for the Senators. The Leafs had eliminated them four times, and they had under-performed several other years. So, just because the team had done well in the regular season didn't mean the team was going to excel in the "second season." Yet, buoyed by the optimism of coach Bryan Murray, the goaltending of Emery, and the scoring of Heatley, that's exactly what happened. The Sens knocked off Pittsburgh in five games in the first round, an impressive win given the high-octane, no-fear style of Sidney Crosby and the Pens. In the next round, they faced a much tougher foe in New Jersey. Martin Brodeur was the best goalie in the game, and the Devils played a style of hockey that, while deathly dull, won championships. The Senators not only won that series, they won it convincingly in five games, and Emery outplayed Brodeur who had, perhaps, the worst playoff series of his career.

Up next was Buffalo, the team that had wiped the Senators from the 2006 playoffs in five routine games. In the interim, though, the Senators had thumped the Sabres during the regular season and were playing with a confidence they had never before had in the playoffs. The result was another five-game series. Ottawa won the first three games to establish control, and won the final game in overtime. For the first time in modern Senators' history, Ottawa was on its way to the Stanley Cup finals.

It was there that they played Anaheim, however, a team with three great defencemen—Chris Pronger, Scott Niedermayer, Francois Beauchemin—a great scorer in Teemu Selanne, and a phenomenal young line in Ryan Getzlaf-Corey Perry-Dustin Penner. The Senators could not match the Ducks for speed, puck pressure, and capitalizing on scoring chances. The Ducks won the Cup. But in defeat, the Senators proved to themselves and their fans that they could make it this far, and with a team in its prime, chances are very good they'll be back in the finals soon, this time perhaps to hold Lord Stanley's mug high.

Andrew Podnieks

Organization

Executive
Eugene Melnyk   Owner, Governor, Chairman
Roy Mlakar   President, CEO, Alternate Governor
Cyril Leeder   Chief Operating Officer
John Muckler   General Manager
Tom Conroy   V.P. & Executive Director, Scotiabank Place
Cheryl Blake   Executive Assistant to President/CEO
Gain Martineau   Executive Assistant to COO

Hockey Operations
Kevin Billet   Director of Hockey Administration
Bryan Murray   Head Coach
Anders Hedberg   Director of Player Personnel/Pro Scout
Frank Jay   Director of Amateur Scouting
John Paddock   Assistant Coach
Greg Carvel   Assistant Coach
Randy Lee   Conditioning Coach
Ron Low   Goaltending Coach/Pro Scout
Tim Pattyson   Video Coach
Rhonda Wing   General Counsel
Heather Havelock   Law Clerk
Allison Vaughan   Assistant to General Manager
Chad Schella   Director of Player Services
Alex Lepore   Team Services/Scouting Coordinator
Gerry Townend   Head Athletic Therapist
Andy Playter   Assistant Athletic Therapist
Scott Allegrino   Equipment Manager
Chris Cook   Assistant Equipment Manager

Scouting Department
Vaclav Burda   Czech Republic/Slovakia
Mikko Ruutu   Finland
Boris Shagas   Russia
Gord Bell, Nick Polano   Pro Scouts
Wayne Daniels, George Fargher, Bob Janecyk,
Bob Lowes, Bill McCarthy, Lewis Mongelluzzo,
Patrick Savard   Scouts

Communications & Publications
Phil Legault   Vice-President, Communications
Steve Keogh   Director, Communications
Karen Ruttan   Director, Publications
Brian Morris   Communications & Publications Coordinator
Eric Tremblay   Translator
Todd Anderson   Content Editor

Broadcasting
Jim Steel   Vice-President, Broadcasting

Corporate & Ticket Sales and Service
Mark Bonneau   Senior Vice-President, Corporate & Ticketing Sales
Brooke Girard   Executive Assistant to Senior Vice-President, Corporate & Ticketing Sales
Bill Courchaine   Director, Corporate Sales
Steve Chesnut, Mark Clatney   Senior Corporate Account Managers
Gina Hillcoat   Director, Business Development
Jim Orban   Director, Sales
Chris Atack   Manager, Inside Sales
Jim Armstrong   Senior Account Manager, Group Sales
Devon Wingate   Account Manager, Group Sales
Matt Berezowski, David Chadala, Chad Elliott,
Jodi Gibson, David Jelley, David Leblanc,
Mark Morrison, Brad Weir, Chris Zito   Account Managers
Jason Dashnay, Gianni Farinon, Joe Lowes,
Phil Murphy, Tim Williton   Corporate Account Managers
Christine Clancy   Director, Premium Services
Tracey Bonner   Manager, Premium Client Services
Deborah Wilson-Desormeaux   Corporate Event Account Manager

Finance
Erin Crowe   Chief Financial Officer
Derek Winch   Controller
Chris Dangerfield   Accounting Manager, Ottawa Senators

Information Technology
Sean Shrubsole   Director, Information Technology
Stephane Bourbonnaais   Web Developer

Marketing
Jeff Kyle   Vice-President, Marketing
Kathy Downs   Administrative Assistant, Marketing
Patti Zebchuck   Director, Marketing
Glen Gower   Director, Game Entertainment
Wendy Moenig   Art Director
Isabelle Perrault-Lachapelle   Director, E-Marketing
Krista Pogue   Director, Media & Scotiabank Place Marketing
Aaron Robinson   Director, Fan & Community Development

Operations & Events
Tom Conroy   Vice-President & Executive Director, Scotiabank Place
Linda Julian   Assistant to Vice-President & Executive Director, Scotiabank Place
Ed Healy   Director, Engineering & Operations

Ottawa Senators Foundation
Dave Ready   President
Colleen Clark   Executive Assistant & Special Events Officer
Danielle Robinson   Director, Corporate & Community Relations

People Department
Sandi Horner   Director, People Department

The Birth of the Ottawa Senators

The Ottawa Senators were original members of the NHL dating back to 1917. The team remained in the league for some 17 years, winning four Stanley Cups during the league's early days—1919-20, 1920-21, 1922-23, and 1926-27. The team became increasingly financially unstable, though, and by the early 1930s it was forced to sell its best players, most notably King Clancy to Toronto in 1930. By 1934, operating a team was no longer feasible and the franchise moved to St. Louis where it assumed the nickname Eagles. After just one season, though, the team folded.

Incredibly, it took 70 years before Ottawa's hopes of getting back into the NHL seemed realistic. On June 12, 1989, Bruce Firestone, chairman of Terrace Investments, filed a letter of intent with the NHL to begin the application process for an expansion franchise. Firestone's vision included a new arena seating 22,500 to be built in Kanata, a thriving area outside Ottawa. The building would be called the Palladium.

In August 1990, the application was formalized when Terrace Investments delivered an 800-page application as well as a cheque for $100,000. That December, an incredible 15,000 people put $25 toward season tickets in a show of support for the franchise. On December 6, 1990, Firestone's dream became a reality when NHL president John Ziegler awarded NHL teams to Ottawa and Tampa Bay for play commencing with the 1992-93 season.

The team adopted its old nickname, the Senators, and played out of the small Civic Centre until the Palladium was completed. It sold 9,100 season tickets in the first week and a half. Meanwhile, to appease residents of Kanata, Firestone reduced his Palladium plans, limiting capacity to 18,500 seats over worries about traffic.

On August 30, 1991, the team made its first hockey operations move by naming Mel Bridgman its general manager. On June 15, 1992, Bridgman unveiled Rick Bowness as the Senators' first head coach, and three days later they selected goalie Peter Sidorkiewicz with the first choice in the Expansion Draft. Notable names selected that day when the roster was filled out included Sylvain Turgeon, Laurie Boschman, and Darren Rumble.

The Senators played their first game on October 8, 1992, a 5-3 home win over Montreal. In August 1993, Firestone sold his interests in the team to Rod Bryden who took over the lengthy process of building the team's arena. On January 17, 1996, the Senators played their first game at the Palladium, losing to Montreal, 3-0. Just five weeks later, the arena was re-named the Corel Centre. On January 19, 2006, it was re-named Scotiabank Place.

Workers put the finishing touches on the Palladium, the first name of Ottawa's new arena but the same building as Scotiabank Place.

Training Camp Roster

Name	Primary 2006-07 Team
Daniel Alfredsson	Ottawa Senators (NHL)
Jamie Allison	Binghamton Senators (AHL)
Michal Barinka	Vitkovice (Czech league)
Cody Bass	Mississauga/Saginaw (OHL)
Danny Bois	Binghamton Senators (AHL)
Charlie Cook	Binghamton Senators (AHL)
Joe Corvo	Ottawa Senators (NHL)
Patrick Eaves	Ottawa Senators (NHL)
Andrew Ebbett	Binghamton Senators (AHL)
Ray Emery	Ottawa Senators (NHL)
Mike Fisher	Ottawa Senators (NHL)
Chanse Fitzpatrick	Phoenix Roadrunners (ECHL)
Nick Foligno	Sudbury Wolves (OHL)
Martin Gerber	Ottawa Senators (NHL)
Denis Hamel	Ottawa Senators (NHL)
Dany Heatley	Ottawa Senators (NHL)
Andy Hedlund	Binghamton Senators (AHL)
Jeff Heerema	Binghamton Senators (AHL)
Josh Hennessy	Binghamton Senators (AHL)
Chris Kelly	Ottawa Senators (NHL)
Neil Komadoski	Binghamton Senators (AHL)
Tomas Kudelka	Lethbridge Hurricanes (WHL)
Arttu Luttinen	Binghamton Senators (AHL)
Tomas Malec	Binghamton Senators (AHL)
Brian Maloney	Binghamton Senators (AHL)
Dean McAmmond	Ottawa Senators (NHL)
Brian McGratton	Ottawa Senators (NHL)
Andrej Meszaros	Ottawa Senators (NHL)
Chris Neil	Ottawa Senators (NHL)
Serge Payer	Binghamton Senators (AHL)
Cory Pecker	Binghamton Senators (AHL)
Neil Petruic	Binghamton Senators (AHL)
Chris Phillips	Ottawa Senators (NHL)
Grant Potulny	Binghamton Senators (AHL)
Tom Preissing	Ottawa Senators (NHL)
Wade Redden	Ottawa Senators (NHL)
Bobby Robins	Binghamton Senators (AHL)
Jean-Claude Sawyer	Cape Breton Screaming Eagles (QMJHL)
Peter Schaefer	Ottawa Senators (NHL)
Christoph Schubert	Ottawa Senators (NHL)
Jason Spezza	Ottawa Senators (NHL)
Antoine Vermette	Ottawa Senators (NHL)
Ryan Vesce	Binghamton Senators (AHL)
Anton Volchenkov	Ottawa Senators (NHL)

Ottawa's first-round draft choice in 2006, Nick Foligno, tries on his new togs during the Entry Draft proceedings in Vancouver on June 24, 2006.

2006-07 Season in Review

Game 1
October 4, 2006
Ottawa 4 at Toronto 1

The Senators began their '06-'07 season with another convincing win over the Leafs, their provincial nemesis who have given them so many troubles in the playoffs. It was Ottawa's eighth win in the last nine games against Toronto, and this was done in fine fashion on several counts. First, goalie Martin Gerber played a solid game. He was signed in the summer to replace Dominik Hasek, who returned to Detroit. Second, it was done on the road, at the hostile Air Canada Centre. And third, it was done with solid defence despite the absence of Zdeno Chara, who signed with Boston in the off-season. The Sens got goals from four different scorers (two with the man advantage) and surrendered just the one goal, that coming from Mats Sundin on a penalty shot after he was hauled down by Anton Volchenkov from behind on a clear break. By that time it was 3-0, but despite the goal the Leafs were unable to rally and the Sens stood tall. In pre-game ceremonies, the Leafs honoured three former greats: the legendary player and coach, Hap Day (number 4); the redhead, Red Kelly (also number 4); and, the pioneering defenceman, Borje Salming (number 21).

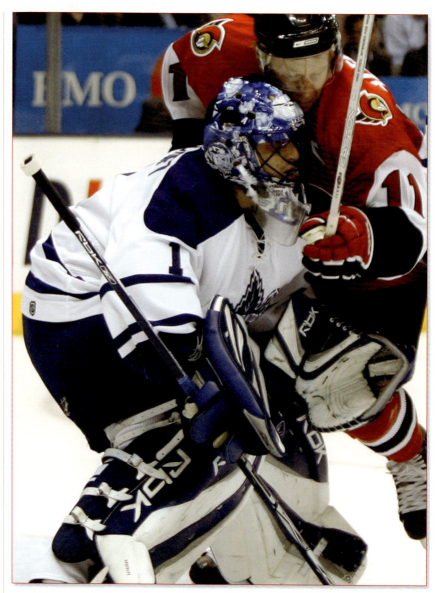
Daniel Alfredsson goes hard to the net against Toronto goalie Andrew Raycroft.

Game 2
October 5, 2006
Toronto 6 at Ottawa 0

Wow. What a reversal of overnight fortunes! The Leafs, who had looked so inferior to their opponents at home, turned the tables on the Senators and dominated from first to last, building a 2-0 lead after 20 minutes and a 5-0 advantage after two periods. They opened the game with a short-handed goal midway through the first period by Chad Kilger and never looked back. Andrew Raycroft got his first win and shutout for his new team and coach Paul Maurice also got his first win with the Leafs. For Ottawa, all the team could do was forget the score and look ahead. Ray Emery got into his first game, replacing a battered Martin Gerber to start the third period. The huge opening night crowd of 19,237 at Scotiabank Place went home disappointed, but the season was still in its infancy.

Game 3

October 7, 2006
Buffalo 4 at Ottawa 3

The Sabres won for the third straight time to start the season, and the Senators lost their second in a row on home ice despite a valiant attempt to make a game of it. They trailed 2-0 after the first, thanks to Henrik Tallinder's goal just 33 seconds from the opening faceoff, and a goal in the final minute by Brian Campbell. Dean McAmmond scored the only goal of the middle period to draw the Sens close, but that was the story of the night—close but no tie. In the third, Jason Spezza scored two goals, but the Senators allowed a goal first in each instance. He made it 3-2 after the Sabres opened another two-goal lead, and he got his second of the period just ten seconds after a Jason Pominville goal had made it 4-2. Despite taking 14 shots on Martin Biron in the final 20 minutes, the Senators couldn't tie the game. It was the Sabres who had eliminated Ottawa from the previous spring's playoffs in five convincing games, and the two division rivals were set to meet eight times this regular season.

Game 4

October 12, 2006
Calgary 1 at Ottawa 0

It surely was too early in the year to panic, but a third loss in succession—all at home—was certainly cause for concern in the nation's capital. This time, it was a lack of offense, a great performance by Calgary goalie Miikka Kiprusoff, and a goal midway through the third period by Jarome Iginla that proved Ottawa's undoing. Kiprusoff stopped all 33 shots, including 17 in the third period, to ensure the victory. More troubling, the Sens went without a goal on six power plays, leaving them a woeful 1-for-25 in the first four games of the season. They were now 0-for-17 at home with the extra man. Ray Emery made the start for Ottawa—his first of the year—and was Kiprusoff's equal, with one exception. Iginla got a backhander away when he claimed a loose puck to Emery's back side, and his shot hit the net for the only goal of the game. The last time the Flames recorded a shutout against Ottawa was on January 15, 1994.

Calgary's Andrew Ference gets tangled up in front of the goal with Chris Neil.

Antoine Vermette makes the moves on Cristobal Huet during Ottawa's 3-2 overtime win against Montreal.

Game 5

October 14, 2006
Ottawa 3 at Montreal 2 (SO)

Despite blowing leads of 1-0 and 2-1, the Senators prevailed in a shootout to break a three-game losing streak, defeating the Canadiens at the Bell Centre before a raucous opening game crowd of 21,273. Antoine Vermette and Mike Fisher were the unlikely heroes of the penalty-shot contest while Ray Emery stopped the two Montreal shootout shots. Chris Higgins and Saku Koivu failed for the Canadiens, while Vermette made a nifty backhand through Cristobal Huet's pads on a deke and Fisher's shot beat the goalie cleanly. Denis Hamel opened the scoring for Ottawa on a backhand that Huet might like to have back, but the Habs tied the game on a short-handed goal from Chris Higgins who made a nice steal of the puck at centre ice and walked in alone on Emery. His hard shot beat the goalie over the glove. The Senators went ahead again before the end of the period when Chris Kelly made a great deflection of a Patrick Eaves' pass at the crease. Most of the rest of the game was evenly played, but the Canadiens earned a point in the standings with a goal late in the third period. Sergei Samsonov scored at 16:37 with a bad-angle shot that beat Emery through the pads, the only weak moment of the game for the goalie. He more than made up for the play with a great effort in the shootout.

Game 6

October 19, 2006
Colorado 2 at Ottawa 1

No one could have predicted that after four home games the Senators would be winless, but that's the position the team was in after dropping another decision, this to Colorado. To make matters worse, the team's power play had another doughnut night on three chances, bringing the scoreless drought to 33 consecutive man advantages without a goal. On the positive side, 50-goal scorer Dany Heatley got his first of the year in the third period to draw the Senators to within a goal, but that's as close as they got. His wrist shot was only partially stopped by Jose Theodore.

After a scoreless first period, the Avalanche broke the game open with two goals on 20 shots in the middle period. Joe Sakic made a great deflection of an Andrew Brunette pass from behind the net despite being checked by two Ottawa players. Brad Richardson doubled the lead while Ottawa was on the power play, and these goals proved enough for the two points. Joe Corvo, an off-season signing by the Senators, made his debut with Ottawa after missing the start of the year recovering from a broken foot.

Game 7

October 21, 2006
New Jersey 1 at Ottawa 8

Few things are as rare in the NHL as scoring enough goals on New Jersey goalie Martin Brodeur to chase him from the net, and just as rare is a night when the defensive-minded Devils surrender eight goals in a game. Yet both of these events occurred at the hands of the Senators, who won for the first time on home ice in a huge way. Even better, the team opened the scoring on the power play midway through the first, courtesy of Jason Spezza. It was only the second power-play goal for the team all year. Although New Jersey tied the game 1-1 on a Brian Gionta score, Ottawa re-took the lead before the end of the first period and blew the game open with five goals in the second. Brodeur was replaced by seldom-used backup Scott Clemmensen, who surrendered the final two goals, but by then the damage had been done. Antoine Vermette and Dean McAmmond both had two goals, while Spezza had two assists to go with his goal. Ray Emery was the winning goalie for Ottawa. The last time the Devils gave up as many goals was in December 1993, nearly 13 years ago.

Chris Neil celebrates a goal against Martin Brodeur and the Devils during a lop-sided 8-1 Sens victory.

Game 8

October 24, 2006
Ottawa 6 at Toronto 2

Avenging a bad 6-0 loss in their second game of the young season, the Senators handed the Leafs a loss of similar proportions right at the Air Canada Centre. Mike Fisher scored just 2:42 into the game, converting a two-on-one with Tom Preissing, and by the midway point of the second period his team led 5-0. Andrej Meszaros made it 2-0 later in the first, but the backbreaker was a wraparound goal that Andrew Raycroft should have stopped with less than 14 seconds left in the period. That made it 3-0, and the Leafs were deflated coming out to start the second. Ottawa kept pouring the pressure on, and at 5-0 coach Paul Maurice gave Raycroft the hook in favour of J-S Aubin. Although the Leafs answered back with an Ian White goal, and made it 5-2 early in the third, the only competitive edge the Leafs had was in the fighting department. The game had two fights and several pushing and shoving matches, but as the clock wound down the home fans let their Leafs know how they felt. The Senators left town with another regular-season win over their provincial rivals.

Antoine Vermette fails to beat Andrew Raycroft on this play, but the Sens hammered the Leafs nonetheless this night.

winning streak, and it came thanks to a former friend, giant defenceman Zdeno Chara who left Ottawa to sign a lucrative contract with Boston in the summer. It was his power-play goal late in the third period that was the decisive score. After a goalless first period, Dany Heatley put Ottawa in front midway through the second period when he ripped a one-timer off a cross-ice pass on a five-on-three past goalie Tim Thomas from the top of the right circle. The lead held up until midway through the third period when defenceman Tom Preissing was stripped of the puck by P-J Axelsson. He walked in alone on Martin Gerber and ripped a shot to the corner over the goalie's glove. That set the stage for Chara who hammered a slapshot from the point past the screened goalie. It was the first power-play goal on the road that Ottawa had surrendered all year, and it was the game winner. Boston had won only two of its first six games.

Game 9

October 26, 2006
Toronto 2 at **Ottawa 7**

Unlike the first two games of the year when Toronto followed up a loss to Ottawa with a convincing win, the Senators matched a lop-sided win in Toronto with an ever more lop-sided one for the home crowd at Scotiabank Place. This time, it was five goals in the second period that paved the road to victory after a first in which Ottawa had the only goal. That was scored by Mike Fisher on a delayed penalty to the Leafs as he swept a loose puck past Andrew Raycroft. Early in the second, Ottawa scored twice in 17 seconds to take a 3-0 lead, but Toronto chipped away and fought back to make it 3-2 halfway through the game. Undaunted, the Senators poured three more shots past Raycroft before the game had reached 40 minutes, and they coasted to victory. There were a plethora of big nights for Ottawa. Joe Corvo and Jason Spezza each had five points on the night, and Dany Heatley had a hat trick—all in the second period and all assisted by Spezza—to signal his return to scoring form. Corvo, a new member of the team in the off-season, set a team record for points by a defenceman with his one goal and four assists. Spezza set his own team record by compiling four assists in that wild second period. Ottawa outshot the Leafs, 40-31.

Game 10

October 28, 2006
Ottawa 1 at **Boston 2**

Just as the Senators seemed to be building momentum, they stumbled, dropping a close road decision to the Bruins after taking a 1-0 lead into the third period. It ended a three-game

Game 11

October 31, 2006
Ottawa 2 at **Montreal 4**

Ottawa's power play was hurting the team not just for lack of scoring but also for allowing short-handed goals against. Tonight the Sens went 0-for-7 with the extra man and gave up a critical goal to Chris Higgins to open the scoring early in the second period. In all, Ottawa had just six goals on 64 chances through eleven games this year. Montreal made it 2-0 later in the period with its new Russian line, Alex Kovalev scoring the goal on assists from Sergei Samsonov and Alexander Perezhogin, the key pass coming from Samsonov as Kovalev skated hard to the goal for the re-direct. Jason Spezza cut the lead to 2-1 early in the third, but the Canadiens played well defensively and weren't in much danger of losing the lead.

Chris Higgins slips the puck through Ray Emery's pads to give Montreal a 1-0 lead in the second period.

Andrei Markov scored into the empty net to make it 3-1, and the teams exchanged last-minute goals that had little effect on the outcome. Ray Emery, who was slowly establishing himself as the team's number-one goalie, started again for Ottawa.

Game 12
November 4, 2006
Carolina 3 at Ottawa 2

For the second time in three games, the Senators blew a lead going into the third period, this time a 2-1 advantage built up thanks to goals by Daniel Alfredsson and Denis Hamel. It was their fifth loss in seven home games and prompted a private team meeting after the game. This despite goalie Martin Gerber receiving his Stanley Cup ring from his old general manager in Carolina, Jim Rutherford, earlier in the afternoon. The loss was hardly Gerber's fault, though. Alfredsson opened the scoring early in the first with a shot over Cam Ward's glove hand, and Hamel made it 2-0 early in the second. The rest of the game was dominated by the Hurricanes. They closed the gap at 15:03 on a power-play goal from Erik Cole, assisted by Rod Brind'Amour. It was Brind'Amour's 1,000th career point. Carolina then scored the only two goals of the final period, both from Ray Whitney, both assisted by Cole. The second of those came midway through the third on a power play with two Senators in the box. Ottawa had had its own lengthy five-on-three earlier in the third and failed to capitalize. In fact, the extra-man woes continued as they failed to score on seven man-advantage situations this night.

Mike Fisher lets go a shot as the Thrashers' Greg de Vries watches.

leads they frittered away against the Thrashers. Slava Kozlov scored the hat trick for the home team. Atlanta fought back from deficits of 1-0, 3-1, and 4-2 to score the only two goals of the third period and claim a 5-4 win. Jason Spezza had a goal and assist in the first period as the Sens headed to the dressing room with a 2-1 lead. Atlanta's only goal was off a short-handed breakaway by Brad Larsen. Daniel Alfredsson scored Ottawa's second goal on the power play, ending an 0-for-16 slump in recent games. Chris Kelly made it 3-1 and then Kozlov scored on a five-on-three for the Thrashers. Atlanta coach Bob Hartley changed goalies after Antoine Vermette made it 4-2, pulling Johan Hedberg and inserting Kari Lehtonen, who stopped all 19 shots he faced. Early in the third, Ilya Kovalchuk's hard wrist shot eluded Martin Gerber to tie the game and then Kozlov completed the hat trick with a goal midway through with the game-winning goal.

Game 13

November 6, 2006
Ottawa 3 at Washington 4 (OT)

Mired in a slump that had now reached four games, the Senators hit a new low this season by building a 3-0 lead in the first period and then giving it all away with an overtime loss to the Capitals. What's worse, they allowed a power-play goal in the final minute to give the Caps a chance to win in the short fourth period. This was not the way to start a four-game road trip. The Sens came out storming the net of Olaf Kolzig, and in the first 12 minutes they got goals from Daniel Alfredsson, Antoine Vermette, and Dany Heatley. Washington coach Glen Hanlon called a timeout and inserted backup Brent Johnson, and the team responded. Ottawa tried to play too conservatively, and Matt Pettinger's late first-period goal gave the Capitals some life. Alexander Ovechkin scored in the second and then again with Johnson on the bench late in the third. In the overtime, Chris Clark converted an Alexander Semin pass at 1:33 to rob the Senators of what should have been a routine two-point night given their blistering start. Semin had three assists for the winners.

Game 14

November 8, 2006
Ottawa 4 at Atlanta 5

Playing better but still having trouble finishing what they started, the Sens lost their fifth in a row, again blowing a lead. Tonight it was three

Game 15

November 10, 2006
Ottawa 6 at Pittsburgh 3

The Senators might have chosen an easier opponent to snap their five-game losing streak against, the longest streak of failure for the team in ten years. Yet going into Pittsburgh and facing Sidney Crosby and Evgeni Malkin, Ottawa did just that, breaking a 2-2 tie game in the second period with three goals in a row en route to the win. In the process, the team handed the Penguins their fourth successive loss, and it was the seventh win in a row over the past three years by the Sens over Pittsburgh. More important, Ottawa managed to hold a lead for the first time in four games, their previous three losses coming after heading into the third period

Pittsburgh's Colby Armstrong crashes Martin Gerber's net.

up at least one goal. Dany Heatley opened the scoring early when Wade Redden spotted him alone to the side of goalie Marc-Andre Fleury, but Michel Ouellet's power-play goal a few minutes later tied the game. The teams exchanged goals later in the first and early in the second before the Sens broke the game open with three in a row. Andrej Meszaros started the run with a shot from the point after the Penguins were unable to clear a bouncing puck from in front. Wade Redden scored with the man advantage, a rarity for the league's 29th-ranked power-play team heading into the game, and Peter Schaefer made it 5-2 early in the third. Heatley put the icing on the cake later after the Pens had made it 5-3. Crosby was limited to a single assist and Malkin to one goal, but neither player factored into their team's offence tonight despite a sellout crowd at the Igloo. Martin Gerber got the start for Ottawa as Ray Emery nursed a sprained forearm.

Game 16

November 11, 2006
Ottawa 3 at Boston 4

Concluding their road trip on a Saturday night after playing the previous night, the Sens faded in the third period and lost a one-goal decision to the Boston Bruins, 4-3. The result wasted a fine rally from 3-1 down thanks to Chris Neil. Glen Murray scored twice for the home team, including the opening goal just 23 seconds into the second period after a scoreless 20 minutes to start. The goal came on the power play when Murray flipped home a loose puck after Martin Gerber failed to control a Zdeno Chara slapshot. It was Chara, the former Senators defenceman, who scored the game-winning goal the first time the teams met earlier in the season. Jason Spezza tied the game on the Ottawa power play, only the team's fifth such goal in 50 attempts this season, but Petr Tenkrat and Murray again gave the Bruins a 3-1 lead late in the second. Murray's goal was the 300th of his career and was a bad one for Gerber; the long shot bounced off his stick and trickled in. Tenkrat's goal was his first of the year after being recalled from the minors earlier in the day. Neil gave the Senators life with a goal at 19:09 off the backhand that beat Tim Thomas, and his second goal tied the game early in the third when he tipped in a Peter Schaefer shot. The rally went all for naught after Patrice Bergeron deflected a Brad Stuart shot at 13:49 of the final period. The Sens were unable to rally a second time even when they were given a late power play courtesy of a Stuart holding penalty at 16:25.

Daniel Alfredsson narrowly avoids a hit from the Sabres' Jason Pominville.

Game 17
November 13, 2006
Montreal 6 at Ottawa 3

Despite returning home for the first time in five games, the Senators were playing their third game in four nights and faded badly in the third period, allowing four Montreal goals in the final 20 minutes of a 6-3 loss. The score was tied 1-1 after the first and Montreal led 2-1 after 40 minutes. Two power-play goals against just 31 seconds apart early in the third was Ottawa's undoing, as a 2-1 nailbiter turned into a 4-1 route. Guillaume Latendresse scored both those goals while playing on the team's number-one line with Saku Koivu and Michael Ryder. The Senators tried to rally by scoring twice with the man advantage themselves, but a goal by Mike Johnson salted the game away and brought out the boobirds at Scotiabank Place who felt goalie Martin Gerber might have put in a better game than he did. Alexei Kovalev scored into the empty net for the game's final tally. Mike Komisarek opened the scoring in the first with the Habs' league-leading seventh goal short-handed, but Denis Hamel tied the game later in the first when he deflected an Andrej Meszaros point shot. Montreal was lucky to be in the game at this point, but Cristobal Huet was outstanding in goal, stopping 16 of 17 shots he faced in the opening 20 minutes while Gerber had only seven at his end. Radek Bonk scored the only goal of the second to give Montreal a lead it would never relinquish, firing a shot from close range late in the period after being left alone by the Sens' defence. It was the second straight loss for Ottawa.

Game 18
November 15, 2006
Ottawa 4 at Buffalo 2

With two days off and a road trip not far from home, Ottawa rallied in the third and showed some extra push as the game wore on to pull away from Buffalo with three unanswered goals in the third period. The goals came in all shapes and sizes—short-handed, even strength, power play—and represented only the second win in nine games for the team. Ray Emery was the starting goalie for the first time in more than two weeks. For Buffalo, it was only the team's second regulation loss in the first 18 games. The night started with promise for Buffalo after Daniel Briere stole the puck from Andrej Meszaros in the Ottawa end. His quick slapshot fooled Emery less than six minutes into the first period to make it 1-0 Sabres. Chris Neil tied it for Ottawa with a shot that beat Martin Biron on the power play just a few minutes later. Buffalo regained the lead when Austrian sniper Thomas Vanek scored his team best 12th goal of the year, banging home a rebound early in the second period. It was the only goal of the middle period but also the last signs of life Buffalo showed. Ottawa got stronger and stronger as the game went on. Jason Spezza tied the game early in the third on a deflection with the extra man, and Peter Schaefer gave the Sens their first lead of the night when he made a great deflection of a Daniel Alfredsson shot. The play went to video review, after which it was determined Schaefer's stick was not above the crossbar. It proved to be the game winner. Chris Phillips finished the scoring with a long empty netter with the Sabres on the power play and Biron on the bench for the two-man advantage. It was the first time all year Ottawa won a game in which it had trailed 1-0.

Game 19

November 17, 2006
Ottawa 2 at **New Jersey 3**

Dean McAmmond tries to deflect a shot past Martin Brodeur, but the goalie makes the save on this play.

Unable to build on their impressive win two nights earlier, Ottawa rallied in the third but fell short in the Meadowlands, losing 3-2 after falling behind 3-0 after two periods. The newly-formed line of Jamie Langenbrunner, Zach Parise, and Travis Zajac accounted for all New Jersey goals, and Martin Brodeur was solid in net, avenging an earlier disastrous performance in which he was pulled after six goals in an 8-1 loss. Langenbrunner scored twice in the first to stake the Devils to a 2-0 lead, and Parise scored the only goal of the second to put the game out of reach thanks to a bad giveaway by Daniel Alfredsson in his own end. Zajac assisted on all three goals. Chris Neil gave the Senators a little life at 5:34 of the third when his deflection spoiled Brodeur's shutout, and Alfredsson atoned for his gaffe with a wicked slapshot that beat Brodeur cleanly midway through the period. The Devils allowed just one more shot the rest of the period, though, and skated to victory. There were only 40 shots by both teams all game (23-17 for the Devils), and after three early power-play chances (two for Ottawa) in the first, the game was penalty free until a Brian Gionta minor assessed after the final horn. The loss left Ottawa with a 7-11-1 record, last in the Northeast Division and struggling to find its form and, more important, its confidence.

Game 20

November 18, 2006
Buffalo 1 at **Ottawa 4**

Winning for only the second time after trailing 1-0 in a game, Ottawa rallied for four straight goals to beat the Sabres for the second successive time. The team's only other come-from-behind 1-0 win came against these same Sabres just four days earlier. It was Buffalo's first road loss all year (in eleven games). The 10-0 start was an NHL record for road wins to start a season. Maxim Afinogenov scored the opening goal of the first with less than one second left on the clock. The play started with a faceoff in the Ottawa end, and Afinogenov drilled a loose puck in the slot that beat Ray Emery before the horn sounded. Undaunted, the Senators scored the only goal of the second. Peter Schaefer connected on the power play, beating goalie Ryan Miller to a loose puck and tying the game 1-1. The third period was all Ottawa. The Sens held a 19-9 advantage in shots in a period featuring nine minor penalties. Dany Heatley gave the Sens their first lead at 1:22 on the power play and Antoine Vermette made it 3-1 later in the period. It was Heatley's team-best 11th goal of the young season. Chris Phillips closed out the scoring in dramatic fashion. After taking a penalty for delay of game for shooting the puck over the glass, he came out of the box and took a breakaway pass from Heatley. The defenceman wired a shot past Miller with the flair of a scoring star at 17:17 to ensure the Senators' victory to the delight of 19,770 fans at Scotiabank Place. Miller was the star of the game for the Sabres. Playing in his first game in almost two weeks because of injury, he held his team in the game time and again with fine saves.

Peter Schaefer gathers a loose puck in tight and beats Minnesota goalie Manny Fernandez on the play.

life. Jason Spezza earned his team-high 25th point and Heatley his 24th point by assisting on Kelly's goal. The win gave the team 19 points, not great but good enough to leave the basement of the Northeast Division to Boston.

Game 22

November 22, 2006
Ottawa 3 at Philadelphia 2 (OT)

Wade Redden scored at 4:39 of overtime to give Ottawa its third win in a row for just the second time this year. The win, starting a four-game road trip, was all the more impressive after Philadelphia moved out to a 2-0 lead by the early point of the second period. The winner came off a one-timer after a nice set-up by Mike Fisher who sent a cross-ice pass to Redden. His shot beat goalie Antero Niittymaki cleanly. It was the Flyers' sixth straight loss in what was becoming one of their worst seasons in franchise history. The team was playing without Peter Forsberg, Jeff Carter, and Mike Rathje, all out with injuries, so the team was ripe for the picking, to be sure. Philadelphia got the only goal of the first in the final minute on a fluke play. Petr Nedved sent the puck through the Ottawa crease, but it bounced off an Ottawa skate past a surprised Ray Emery for the early Flyers' lead. They made it 2-0 in the second on an almost equally lucky goal. Emery made a pad save, put the puck bounced up and Mike Knuble batted it out of the air. The team could not take these lucky breaks to the bank, though. Mike Fisher beat Niittymaki with a wrist shot on the power play to make it 2-1 at 8:42 of the second, and Daniel Alfredsson tied the game in the final minute with another wrist shot. There was no scoring in the third, and the game was marked by a paucity of penalties. Philadelphia incurred

Game 21

November 20, 2006
Minnesota 3 at Ottawa 5

Winning for the second time in a row for the first time in nearly four weeks, the Senators took the easier route by storming out of the gate with three first-period goals and hanging on for victory. They got goals from five different scorers and a first-star performance from Ray Emery who stopped 42 of 45 shots he faced, including 18 of 20 in a wild third period. It was a complete reversal of the first period in which the Sens held a wide margin in shots (17-8) and took control of the game. Andrejs Meszaros opened the scoring at 5:04 with a hard wrist shot that beat Manny Fernandez, and Chris Kelly made it 2-0 just over a minute later. Chris Neil scored on the power play against Minnesota's number-one ranked penalty killing to make it 3-0, and Daniel Alfredsson made it 4-0 early in the second. The closest Minnesota came was midway through the third when Brian Rolston beat Emery on a penalty shot to make it a 4-2 game. He was given the free shot after Mike Fisher closed his hand on the puck in the Ottawa crease. The teams exchanged goals late in the game after the result was no longer in question. Ottawa improved its overall record to 9-11-1 and was starting to show signs of only three minors and the Senators had a rare, penalty-free game. That paved the way for Redden's overtime heroics, although the Flyers did earn a precious point in the standings. Peter Schaefer had three assists for the Sens.

Game 23

November 24, 2006
Ottawa 6 at Florida 4

Displaying the scoring power that made the team the top offensive power the previous year, the Senators poured six goals past Florida in a convincing win, their season-high fourth in a row. Dany Heatley led the way with a hat trick and an assist. He recorded a hat trick earlier in the year against Toronto. The win put Ottawa at 11-11-1, the first time in nearly a month it was at .500. Despite the scoring, the Sens needed a third-period push to get by the Panthers. The home team opened the scoring at 7:09 of the first when Stephen Weiss made a great second effort, knocking the puck in from behind the red line while on the ice. Heatley scored the first two Ottawa goals to give the Sens a 2-1 lead after 20 minutes. The first came on a lucky break. Goalie Ed Belfour went behind the net to play a routine shoot-in, but the puck took a weird bounce off the boards and came right in front of the open net. Heatley merely had to snap it into the vacated goal. His second was a more legitimate effort. Belfour stopped a Jason Spezza shot on the power play, but Heatley was at the crease to knock in the rebound. Dean McAmmond gave the Sens a 3-1 lead and seemed to give his team momentum, but the Panthers fought back, scoring the next three goals. They tied the game 3-3 before the end of the second and took the lead early in the third on a Gary Roberts power-play goal at 3:29, but Ottawa responded with the final three goals of the game. Mike Fisher started the rally by redirecting a Patrick Eaves pass beautifully behind Belfour. Spezza got the eventual winner on the power play less than two minutes later and Heatley completed his three-goal night with a marker with a minute left to play.

Tampa Bay defenceman Dan Boyle erases Mike Fisher from the play along the boards.

Game 24

November 26, 2006
Ottawa 1 at **Tampa Bay 3**

With a chance to move into eighth place in the Eastern Conference, the Senators came up short. Unable to build on or hold a 1-0 lead after 20 minutes, they lost for the first time in five games thanks to a superior goaltending performance from the Lightning's Johan Holmqvist. It was the first win by Tampa Bay over Ottawa in nine games over a three-year period. Jason Spezza gave Ottawa the lead just 3:34 into the game on a hard slapshot, yet this proved to be the only shot that would beat Holmqvist all night. The Lightning exploded for two quick goals midway through the second to take the lead, and Ottawa couldn't rally to tie. It was during the latter half of the second, with the score 2-1, that Holmqvist made his finest stops, notably on a post-to-post stop off Joe Corvo. Filip Kuba had scored first for Tampa Bay, at 10:28, and Brad Richards scored just 36 seconds later. Richards's shot was a trademark bullet to the top corner over Emery's glove. Martin St. Louis scored a late power-play goal in the third period to ensure the win which sent the Senators below .500 again (11-12-1). Jason Spezza was in the box after taking a hooking penalty. There were only six minor penalties called all game (four against Ottawa), and the Senators had the advantage in shots, 23-18. It may have been a loss in the standings, but the Sens left the rink feeling they had played well enough to win.

Carolina goalie John Grahame fails to stop Mike Fisher from scoring.

Game 25

November 28, 2006
Ottawa 4 at Carolina 1

Despite falling behind early, the Senators remained patient and rallied for a big win against the previous year's Stanley Cup champions. Martin Gerber got the start in goal for Ottawa, his first start in eight games. But it was a motivational strategy by coach Bryan Murray, for Gerber was part of the Hurricanes the previous year. In fact, he set a team record in 2005-06 with 38 wins during the regular season before being signed by the Senators as a free agent during the summer. The last time he was in Carolina, he was hoisting the Stanley Cup, but Gerber was returning as an opponent now. Murray's strategy worked, and Gerber stopped 29 of 30 shots. He had been the losing goalie in five of his previous six appearances. Although Carolina got the first goal just 2:30 into the game off an Andrew Ladd shot, the Senators came right back and tied the score when Patrick Eaves chipped home a loose puck near John Grahame's crease. Gerber settled down after that goal and played with confidence the rest of the night. At the other end, Grahame kept the score close in a period his team was outshot, 17-7, but Ottawa kept coming in the second. Christoph Schubert scored on a long slapshot early in the middle period for a 2-1 lead. It was a shot the goalie might normally have saved. Mike Fisher made it 3-1 on a rush off the counter attack, and Chris Neil finished the scoring with a tip-in of a Dany Heatley shot midway through the third. The win was the fifth in the last six games for Ottawa while Carolina suffered its third loss in four games.

Game 26

November 30, 2006
Florida 0 at **Ottawa 6**

Showing a power that the fans had expected all year, the Ottawa Senators played their best game of the season in hammering Florida 6-0, dominating every aspect of the game and entertaining the crowd of 17,814 at Scotiabank Place. They scored three times in each of the first two periods and played on cruise control in the third. Ray Emery had the shutout, stopping all 31 Panthers' shots. It was the third straight game the Panthers had been shut out. Alexander Auld started the game but was pulled after allowing five goals over the first 26:01 of the game. Ed Belfour came in and allowed the final Ottawa goal. Dany Heatley started the scoring spree early on a power play. A shot off the end boards came out in front, and his quick backhand swat floated over Auld for the early 1-0 lead. He then scored his 16th goal of the year a few minutes later and Mike Fisher made it 3-0 late in the first. Chris Kelly made it 4-0 early in the second, and then Andrej Meszaros, who led all Senators with 22:34 of ice time, made it 5-0. Antoine Vermette closed out the scoring. Emery had his greatest challenge in the third period but he stopped all 14 shots he faced and earned his fourth career shutout. Despite the score, in fact, it was Florida which held an advantage in shots, 31-28. The game was delayed several minutes in the first period after Chris Phillips took Stephen Weiss hard into the boards, breaking a sheet of Plexiglas and sending two children to the hospital with minor cuts.

Game 27

December 2, 2006
Tampa Bay 2 at Ottawa 5

The Senators roared to a 4-0 first-period lead and then coasted to a relatively easy win over Tampa Bay before 18,618 contented fans at Scotiabank Place. The win was highlighted by two goals from Antoine Vermette, the first of which was one of the most inventive and amazing goals of the year. Standing to the glove side of goalie Johan Holmqvist behind the end red line, back to the goalie, Vermette moved the puck out front and put his stick between his legs. He flipped the puck in on the short side before Holmqvist could cover the post, all the while remaining behind the goal line. The play happened in the blink of an eye. The goal was enough for Tampa Bay coach John Tortorella who yanked Holmqvist and inserted Karri Ramo, who was playing in his first career NHL game. Ottawa got on the board first with an early short-handed goal. Patrick Eaves stole the puck at the Lightning blueline and made no mistake on his quick break. Four minutes later, Joe Corvo made it 2-0 on the power play before Vermette made his great move. Jason Spezza rounded out the first-period barrage. Tampa Bay controlled most of the second period, scoring twice and having three power plays to close the gap to a goal, but Ray Emery stood tall in the Ottawa nets when he had to. Over the final 40 minutes, shots were 29-14 for Tampa, but the team had put itself in too big a hole to crawl out of on this night. Vermette had the only goal of the third period to make it a 5-2 game. Ottawa now had a 5-5 record at home.

Antoine Vermette scores on Karri Ramo in the goalie's first NHL game after replacing Johan Holmqvist.

Game 28

December 5, 2006
Ottawa 4 at NY Islanders 2

The Senators' season seemed finally to be rounding nicely into shape. Dany Heatley opened and closed the scoring; the Sens jumped into another early lead; and, Martin Gerber played a solid game in goal spelling Ray Emery for the night. As a result, the team won for the fourth time in a row and eighth time in the last nine games. The Islanders were without captain Alexei Yashin and they also started their backup goalie, Mike Dunham, to give starter Rick DiPietro a night off. Dunham was busy, stopping 31 of 35 shots. Jason Spezza had a goal (his 13th of the year) and two assists, the first helper setting up Heatley for the game's first goal just 4:32 from the opening faceoff. His hard shot on the power play late in the period made it 2-0 in a period dominated by Ottawa. The Sens outshot the Islanders 17-4 in the opening period, and only some fine work by Dunham kept the score close. Andy Hilbert made it a 2-1 game midway through the second, but a great pass from Daniel Alfredsson to Joe Corvo to the back door of Dunham on an Ottawa man advantage restored the two-goal lead. The teams exchanged goals in the third as well, but Ottawa played solid defence and never seemed in danger or relinquishing the lead. The win put the team sixth in the Eastern Conference standings, but it was not without cost. Captain Daniel Alfredsson left the game early in the third and didn't return, and he was out of the lineup for an undetermined period.

The Rangers' Marek Malik takes his man, Ottawa's Antoine Vermette, lifting the goal off the ice in the process.

Game 29

December 6, 2006
Ottawa 2 at Washington 6

Playing without Daniel Alfredsson, the Senators were easy prey for the hot Washington Capitals who won their fourth game in a row and second of the year against Ottawa. Chris Clark had two goals for the winners and Alexander Ovechkin added three assists in his team's cause. The game was marred by 18 minor penalties and two fights which took all flow out of the play, favouring the Caps. Ottawa coach Bryan Murray also suggested after the game that one goal was offside and another should never have happened because of a blown icing call. All in all, it was a game for the Sens to forget. Indeed, Antoine Vermette's giveaway early in the game set the tone for the night. Matt Bradley capitalized on the play by firing a quick shot over Ray Emery's glove at 15:30 to make it 1-0. Just 36 seconds later, Clark scored his first of the night to give the Caps a 2-0 lead after 20 minutes on a play Murray believed Ovechkin was clearly offside. In the second, Ottawa made it close when Mike Fisher scored on the power play, but Clark extended the lead to 3-1 with another goal a few minutes later on a play Murray felt should have been called icing. Jason Spezza tried to ignite an Ottawa rally with a goal early in the third, but Washington pulled away with three unanswered goals to seal the victory. Alexander Semin and Matt Pettinger scored on the power play and Brooks Laich made it 6-2 at 11:45 to close out the scoring. Like Emery, Olaf Kolzig was busy in goal, both men facing 37 shots. Ottawa returned home after its two-game mini-road trip for two days of practice before its next game.

Game 30

December 9, 2006
NY Rangers 3 at Ottawa 1

Despite having only two wins in the previous 12 meetings between the teams, the Rangers managed a matinee win in Ottawa thanks to two great plays by Jaromir Jagr and several fine saves by young netminder Henrik Lundqvist. The Sens were once again without captain Daniel Alfredsson, but the way Lundqvist played Alfredsson's presence might not have made that big a difference. Jagr helped the Rangers get on the board late in the first period on a five-on-three. He whipped a hard pass through Ray Emery's crease right on the tape of Martin Straka who had only to get good wood on the pass to pop it in the open side. Early in the second, Jagr made it 2-0 for New York on a typically great play. He took the puck outside the blueline and turned and twisted his way into the slot, letting go a shot with seemingly impossible velocity that beat Emery cleanly. Later in the period the Sens made it a one-goal game again. Jason Spezza made a nice deflection of a Christoph Schubert point shot with the extra man to beat Lundqvist. The turning point came a short time later when Lundqvist stoned Dany Heatley on a breakaway and on the ensuing action made two more tremendous saves to keep it a 2-1 game after two periods. The save on Heatley was not surprising given that Lundqvist was an incredible 22 for 22 on shootout shots this year. The third period was evenly played, but Brendan Shanahan scored his league-leading 22nd goal into an empty net to seal the win for the Blueshirts.

Game 31

December 10, 2006
Ottawa 2 at **Columbus 6**

Rick Nash scored twice in the first period and Columbus led 5-0 before Ottawa got on the scoreboard in this route at the Nationwide Arena in Ohio. It was the third straight loss for the Sens despite playing a team that was far down in the standings. Penalties were the difference as the Blue Jackets scored five times on eleven power-play chances. Martin Gerber started for Ottawa, but after surrendering four goals on just 13 shots he was replaced by Ray Emery midway through the game. It was not Gerber's finest hour, to be sure. At the other end, Pascal Leclaire started for Columbus and had a shutout going, but he pulled a groin late in the second and was replaced by Fredrik Norrena, making this a rare game in which four goalies played. Nash's first goal of the night was a lucky one. Gerber went behind the net to handle the puck but badly misplayed it, and Nash found himself in the slot with the puck and an empty net. Later in the period, he corralled a loose puck and turned and fired quickly to beat Gerber on the power play to stake the Blue Jackets to an early 2-0 lead. In the second, it was all Columbus on the scoresheet but not in terms of chances. Columbus scored the only three goals to boost their lead to 5-0, but for a bit of Peter Schaefer luck the game might have turned out differently. Leclaire stoned the Ottawa forward on two clear breakaways as well as a penalty shot to keep the shutout going, and Schaefer could only shake his head at what might have been. Christoph Schubert and Mike Fisher made it 5-2 early in the third, but any thoughts of a miraculous rally were dashed when Manny Malhotra made it 6-2 midway through the third.

Patrick Eaves moves into the Columbus end as defenceman Anders Eriksson looks on.

Game 32

December 12, 2006
Ottawa 3 at Detroit 2

After three less-than-impressive losses in a row, Ottawa came back and played a great game against one of the best teams in the league, beating Detroit, 3-2. All goals came in a hectic second period of a game which featured great goaltending. Young Ray Emery bested the grizzled Dominik Hasek who had abandoned the Senators in the off-season to go to the Red Wings for possibly one last season. Ottawa raced into a 3-0 lead early in the second and then held on for dear life. Emery was by far the busier of the goalies, stopping 43 of 45 shots thrown his way at the Joe Louis Arena. Hasek faced only 22 shots. The game was scoreless after the first period thanks only to Emery. Detroit outshot Ottawa 18-3 in the first, so when the Sens headed to the dressing room after 20 minutes they realized how fortunate they were to still have a chance to win. They parlayed that fortune with better play in the middle period. Jason Spezza opened the scoring just 1:44 into the second. He stole the puck at the Detroit blueline and went in alone on Hasek. The goalie felt Spezza didn't quite have control of the puck and made a lunge to pokecheck him, but Spezza calmly moved to the backhand and roofed the puck into the vacated top of the net. That extended his point-scoring streak to an even ten games. Less than four minutes later, Ottawa made it 2-0 on the power play when Chris Neil tipped a Christoph Schubert shot into the net. The man advantage was the result of a Hasek penalty for playing the puck outside the hexagon behind the goal line. A minute and a half later, the Sens made it 3-0 thanks to a great solo effort by Spezza. He dipsy-doodled through the entire Detroit team inside its blueline and fired a rocket past Hasek. Robert Lang and Pavel Datsyuk made it 3-2 before the end of the period, but despite a heavy advantage in play in the third, Detroit couldn't beat Emery for the tying goal.

Defenceman Anton Volchenkov swats the puck out of harm's way.

Game 33

December 14, 2006
Ottawa 0 at **Nashville 6**

There wasn't much good to come out of this game for Ottawa save that it was one night, two points lost, and on the road again to the next destination. Nashville scored three times in the first period, and Steve Sullivan scored three times in the second, to lead the front-running Predators to a resounding six-love win in this tennis set of a game at the Gaylord Entertainment Centre. Sullivan's pure hat trick came in a span of 5:56, a franchise record. He was playing in his first game in a week after recovering from a strained groin. J-P Dumont assisted on all of his goals. Scott Hartnell scored twice for the Predators in the first. Daniel Alfredsson and Wade Redden were still out of the Ottawa lineup—as was Peter Schaefer on this night as well—but the team couldn't use injuries as an excuse to justify this poor a performance. Ray Emery was pulled after allowing all six goals on 14 shots, but he was hardly to blame. Both Hartnell goals, for instance, were the result of great passes from Paul Kariya that left the shooter with nothing but net to hit. The Nashville passing was testament to the team's skill, but it also revealed Ottawa's lack of movement in its own end on this night as too often they were caught flat-footed. Ottawa also took six of the last seven penalties in the game to negate any chance of getting back into it.

Game 34

December 16, 2006
Ottawa 3 at **Buffalo 1**

Since losing to Buffalo in the playoffs the previous spring, Ottawa had done a magnificent job of ensuring there was no psychological fallout. The Sens defeated the Sabres for the third time in a row this season, and Buffalo, one of the hottest teams all year and leading the league in goals scored, had now lost only six games all year—three to Ottawa. Daniel Alfredsson was back in the lineup for Ottawa to help key the win. The Sens jumped into a 2-0 first period lead. Dany Heatley scored at 5:42 when he helped a rolling puck over the goal line. Andrej Meszaros's point shot snuck through Ryan Miller's pads and might have gone in on its own, but Heatley was leaving nothing to chance and netted his 19th of the year. Ottawa doubled the lead when Heatley made a great pass to Jason Spezza on the power play, and his quick shot beat Miller at 17:29. Jochen Hecht scored the only goal of the second to make for an interesting third period, but Spezza clicked again with Heatley and Antoine Vermette on an early power play to put the game out of reach. That goal tied Spezza with Heatley at 19 goals for the team lead. Spezza almost had the hat trick later in the final period but couldn't beat Miller on a penalty shot. Ray Emery stopped 35 of 36 shots he faced in the Ottawa goal. He was especially sharp in a 13-shot second period in which the Sabres also had the only three power plays.

Game 35

December 19, 2006
Boston 7 at **Ottawa 2**

The psychological elements of the game were just as clear tonight as they had been the previous game for Ottawa. Just as the Senators had mastered the art of beating Buffalo, so, too, had the Boston Bruins and their new giant captain, former Sens defenceman Zdeno Chara, learned to master the Sens. For the third time in as many games, it was Chara's new team that beat his old, this the first game he played in Ottawa since defecting to the Bruins as a free agent in the summer. This night's game was no contest. Whatever could go wrong for Ottawa did. Although the fans booed Chara every time he touched the puck, they started to boo their own team, too, as the game went out of reach. Marco Sturm had a hat trick for Boston and Patrice Bergeron accumulated five assists. Boston scored the only three goals of the first period and led 5-0 before Christoph Schubert scored at 19:55 of the second to break the shutout. The game was enlivened by two controversial plays. On the first, Brian McGrattan went after Wayne Primeau in the second period to touch off a melee involving everyone on the ice. Then in the third period, Patrick Eaves was handed a five-minute major and game misconduct for elbowing Marc Savard. If Ottawa was going to lose, it wasn't going down without a fight, but on this night it only turned an ugly game uglier.

(l-r) Daniel Alfredsson, Dany Heatley, and Jason Spezza celebrate a goal against Tampa Bay.

Game 36

December 21, 2006
Tampa Bay 4 at Ottawa 2

Sometimes there is more to a loss than just the numbers on the scoreboard. This was one such game. For starters, the home defeat dropped Ottawa's record to 6-9 at Scotiabank Place, third worst in the league. The Sens lost nine games at home for the entire 2005-06 season. Second, the Sens took a 2-1 lead into the third period, but as had been their habit earlier in the year, that lead fell by the wayside. Third, star forward Jason Spezza left the building on crutches, fuelling worries about a lengthy absence. The only good news was that after a nine-game layoff with a shoulder injury, defenceman Wade Redden was back in the lineup for the Sens. Dany Heatley and Antoine Vermette scored in the second period around a Martin St. Louis goal, but it was all Tampa Bay in the final 20 minutes. Heatley's goal was the result of a nice passing play with the extra man. It was his 20th of the season and 150th of his career. Ruslan Fedotenko tied the game 2-2 early in the third when his long shot beat Ray Emery, and the Lightning went ahead for good at 8:53 when Brad Richards won a faceoff in the Ottawa end back to the point. Defenceman Paul Ranger took a shot that pinballed in front past Emery. Vincent Lecavalier added an empty net goal in the final minute.

Mike Fisher is stopped by Antero Niittymaki of the Flyers on this play, though the Senators won the game easily, 6-3.

Game 37

December 23, 2006
Ottawa 6 at Philadelphia 3

Despite the bleak news that Jason Spezza would be lost to the team for a month, Ottawa had equally positive news in that their final pre-Christmas opponent would be Philadelphia, losers of eight in a row—nine after this game and six at home, both all-time team records for futility. The win gave the Ottawas a decidedly mediocre 18-18-1 record heading into the holiday break, but there was more optimism than not to the first part of the schedule. The newly-formed threesome of Dany Heatley-Daniel Alfredsson-Mike Fisher combined for six points, led by Alfredsson's two goals and assist. Joe Corvo opened the scoring with a one-timer on the power play early on, beating Antero Niittymaki, but the Flyers came back and took a 2-1 lead on goals by Ben Eager and Jeff Carter. The Sens turned the tables on Philadelphia in the second and headed to the dressing room after 40 minutes in a 3-3 tie. Chris Phillips made it 2-2 and then Denis Hamel scored on a breakaway to give the Sens the lead. Kyle Calder responded for the Flyers, but the third period belonged to Ottawa. Heatley stole the puck from Derian Hatcher and his shot was stopped by Niittymaki, but Alfredsson was right there to bang in the rebound for what proved to be the winning goal. Peter Schaefer added an insurance goal and then Alfredsson hit the empty net in the final minute. Ottawa fired 42 shots at Niittymaki while Martin Gerber saw 29 from Philadelphia, the worst team in the league.

Game 38

December 27, 2006
NY Islanders 0 at Ottawa 2

Starting off the post-Christmas schedule on the right note, Ottawa got goals late in the first and third periods and Ray Emery stopped everything he saw for a solid if unspectacular victory, the team's second straight. The game was witnessed by a record 20,192 fans at Scotiabank Place. Just as Emery was earning his second shutout of the year, the Sens were putting an end to Rick DiPietro's shutout string at the other end. The Islanders' number-one goalie had recorded goalless games in each of his last two starts, but Mike Fisher's score at 18:12 of the first put an end to the streak after 156:30 shutout minutes. The goal came after DiPietro overplayed a pass from Daniel Alfredsson to Dany Heatley, and the puck bounced off a skate to Fisher who was alone with the empty net. Chris Kelly added the insurance goal late in the third at the end of a strange series of power plays. The Islanders were assessed three minor penalties at 12:30. Richard Park was fenced for tripping, and at the same time Alexei Yashin was given a hooking penalty. Irate, coach Ted Nolan spoke to the referees in less than polite terms and earned a bench minor. The Isles killed off the two-minute, five-on-three situation, but when Nolan's minor kicked in the Senators capitalized with just one second left in the penalty. Most impressive for Ottawa, the team played well in the second and third periods with the lead, continuing to play hard and playing positionally strong in their own end, but not sitting back and letting the Islanders take the play to them.

Game 39

December 29, 2006
NY Rangers 0 at Ottawa 1

The paradox of playing winning hockey was again evident this night as the Senators won their third game in a row since losing their top scorer, Jason Spezza, to injury. It was a win accomplished through superior defensive effort and more great goaltending from Ray Emery. Daniel Alfredsson scored just 32 seconds after the opening faceoff, and that goal stood up for the next 59-plus minutes. The Rangers lost their seventh game in a row. Emery stopped 27 shots in recording his second straight shutout. As well, the Sens managed to squeeze some 20,214 fans into Scotiabank Place, setting a new attendance record for the second straight night. Alfredsson's goal was a simple tip of a Chris Phillips shot that eluded Henrik Lundqvist. The goal held up thanks to some great penalty killing, notably later in the first when the Sens incurred two minors and a major to Chris Neil, leaving the team down a man for nine minutes during one 13-minute stretch. Neil was given five minutes for charging, hitting Petr Prucha from behind. Mike Fisher missed the game, so the gritty and reliable Chris Kelly was put on the top line with Alfredsson and Dany Heatley.

Game 40

December 30, 2006
Ottawa 3 at Toronto 2 (OT)

Ottawa's fourth win in a row and last of the calendar year 2006 was accomplished in dramatic fashion

Chris Phillips scores the game-winning goal in overtime as Toronto goalie Andrew Raycroft lies helplessly on the ice.

against their fiercest rivals. Chris Phillips scored on a breakaway at 2:39 of overtime to give the Sens a huge two points while the Leafs had to settle for one point by virtue of getting the game into the short fourth period. It was a game the Leafs should have won but didn't. They peppered Ray Emery with 45 shots but had little scoring touch and were bettered by the goalie. At the other end, Andrew Raycroft was hardly stellar for the Leafs in defeat. Toronto scored the only goal of the first on a late power play, Alexander Steen putting the finishing touches on the man-advantage opportunity. It was a period in which Toronto held a 20-9 advantage in shots yet managed just a single goal. Ottawa came back with the only marker of the second, a short-handed effort by Dean McAmmond. He poked in a rebound after Chris Kelly missed on a breakaway and Raycroft couldn't control the rebound. The Leafs had a great chance to take the lead right away, but Tomas Kaberle missed a wide open net on a three-on-two rush. The Leafs did go ahead early in the third when Boyd Devereaux, a recent callup, fired a shot past Emery's blocker. The Leafs were missing nine regulars thanks to a series of injuries that had decimated the lineup. Kelly then tied the game with just 2:06 remaining, ruining a fine Toronto effort and forcing overtime. Phillips' goal came after a great pass by Dany Heatley to spring the defenceman and he made no mistake by beating Raycroft for the win.

Ray Emery gets his glove on the puck to freeze action around his net.

Game 41

January 1, 2007
Atlanta 3 at Ottawa 2 (OT)

It wasn't such a Happy New Year for Ottawa as the Sens lost in overtime after a Slava Kozlov shot eluded Ray Emery at 1:48 of the extra period. Nonetheless, the Sens rallied for a late goal in the third period to earn one important point in the standings. Kozlov had two goals and Marian Hossa, the former Senators forward who was traded for Dany Heatley prior to the previous season, had three assists for the Thrashers, winners of six of their last seven games. It was Ottawa's first loss since Jason Spezza went down with injury and, not surprisingly, it was the result of a weaker than usual defensive effort. Also missing were Mike Fisher and Antoine Vermette. Kari Lehtonen played well in Atlanta's goal, stopping 33 of 35 Ottawa shots. Ray Emery faced 29 shots. Daniel Alfredsson staked Ottawa to a lead in the first minute of the second period on the power play with Brad Larsen in the penalty box. Ilya Kovalchuk tied the game a few minutes later on his patented one-timer slapshot from the point, and Kozlov scored his first of the night midway through the period to give Atlanta the lead. He scooped up a rebound off a Hossa shot before Emery could collect the puck. His overtime goal was a thing of beauty. On a delayed penalty against the Senators, Hossa saw Kozlov and fed him a perfect pass just as Kozlov eluded defenceman Joe Korvo. Kozlov went in alone on Emery, made a little move, and tucked a backhander between the goalie's pads for the game-winning goal.

Game 42

January 3, 2007
Buffalo 3 at **Ottawa 6**

Scotiabank Place was abuzz before the game, during the game, and after, all for different but related reasons. Before the game the talk was all about the big trade. Ottawa landed Mike Comrie from Phoenix the previous day, a skilled forward who could put the puck in the net. During the game, Dany Heatley stole the spotlight by scoring three goals and adding an assist—all in the second period—to ignite a frenzied Ottawa attack that handed Buffalo the fourth loss in five games between the teams this season. After the game, the talk was all about a new team, a new confidence, a new year. Almost lost in the enthusiasm was another great night from goalie Ray Emery who faced 36 Buffalo shots and stopped 33 of them. Ottawa got three of its goals on just four power-play chances. Heatley got the game's first goal at 4:53 of the second by batting a puck out of the air in front of Ryan Miller while short-handed. He made it 2-0 about six minutes later and earned an assist on Tom Preissing's power-play score at 12:20. He capped the period with his team-record-tying fourth point by converting another power play with Derek Roy in the box serving a slashing penalty. It was Heatley's third hat trick of the year, tops in the league. Paul Gaustad got Buffalo on the scoresheet early in the third but the Sens pulled away with two more goals. Comrie ended up with two assists and impressed teammates and fans with his puck-handling ability. Despite the glitter, though, it was Emery who made the romp seem possible. Ottawa was outshot 19-7 in the first 20 minutes, yet the teams headed to the dressing room in a scoreless tie thanks to the Ottawa goalie.

Game 43

January 6, 2007
New Jersey 3 at Ottawa 2

The Senators lost this Saturday matinee to the defensive-minded New Jersey Devils in typical fashion, as the Devils clogged the middle, kept play to the outside, played the trap, and generally did everything to prevent scoring chances. Of course, any talk of New Jersey and allowing few goals starts with Martin Brodeur, and he was also sensational, stopping 33 of 35 shots. Zack Parise gave New Jersey the lead when he took a Travis Zajac pass and snapped it past Ray Emery at 6:13. Ottawa managed to beat the trap long enough to tie the game later in the period on a Patrick Eaves goal. It came off a turnover in the New Jersey end when Dean McAmmond stole the puck from David Hale. Brian Gionta proved the giant killer, though. He scored early in the second by tipping a Hale shot, and again late in the third after capitalizing on an Andrej Meszaros turnover. No team is tougher to play against when it has the lead than the Devils. They not only play the trap, they also manage to stay out of the penalty box and allow few odd-man rushes. Still, the Sens pressed and Brodeur was called upon to make several fine saves, the best off Dany Heatley and Daniel Alfredsson from in close. Tom Preissing made it a one-goal game with less than two minutes to play when he tucked in a rebound, but New Jersey simply kept playing stifling defence and won in regulation time.

Anton Volchenkov collides with New Jersey forward Scott Gomez in a big open-ice collision.

Game 44

January 7, 2007
Philadelphia 1 at Ottawa 6

The Senators were never in jeopardy in this comfortable victory, scoring early and often en route to their second win of 2007. Daniel Alfredsson started and finished the play for the first goal. He controlled the puck along the boards deep in the Philadelphia end, got it back to the point, and then scooped in the rebound at 6:29. Joe Corvo made it 2-0 with Alfredsson's help about ten minutes later. Again, the captain controlled the puck before getting it to the defenceman, and his hard shot beat Antero Niittymaki. R.J. Umberger closed the gap early in the second after eluding Corvo and goalie Martin Gerber to chase down a loose puck, and the Flyers' forward had an empty net once he got control of the puck. This was Gerber's first home start in nearly two months, coach Murray giving the goalie time off from the Scotiabank Place fans after a poor start to his season and subsequent booing from the fans. The Senators responded with three unanswered goals, two from Dany Heatley. The other goal came from Josh Hennessy, his first career NHL goal. Christoph Schubert beat Flyers' defenceman David Printz to the puck and fired a quick shot from a bad angle. Niittymaki made the save but kicked the puck right to the Ottawa rookie who banged it home for the highlight goal. Chris Kelly scored in the third as Ottawa outshot Philadelphia, 43-21. Niittymaki lost his eleventh straight game for the Flyers who were once again without captain Peter Forsberg. The team was now 0-12-3 with him out of the lineup. For the Senators, it was their sixth win in eight games as the team continued its steady climb in the conference standings.

Ottawa's Tom Preissing squeezes Boston forward Wayne Primeau out along the boards.

Game 45

January 9, 2007
Boston 2 at Ottawa 5

Perhaps there was a correlation, but this was the first time in four games that Ottawa had defeated Boston this year, and it was the first of those games in which former Senators' defenceman Zdeno Chara did not play for the Bruins. He missed the game with an injury, and the result was a stark contrast to previous encounters. Boston had the edge in play for the first few minutes of the game and built a 2-0 lead, but the Senators got stronger and stronger and simply hammered the Bruins in the final period, scoring five unanswered goals and roaring away to victory. Marco Sturm opened the scoring at 2:40 in most unusual fashion. He had a breakaway while his team was short-handed and Ottawa defenceman Andrej Meszaros pulled him down, giving Sturm a penalty shot. He made no mistake in beating Ray Emery with a quick deke and high shot. The Bruins made it 2-0 midway through the period when Paul Mara scored. Ottawa failed to capitalize on the only three power plays of the opening period, and the second period was a scoreless one in which teams traded few scoring chances. The Senators came to play in the third, though. Mike Comrie started the scoring spree with an early goal, his first with the team since being acquired in a trade from Phoenix a week ago, and Dany Heatley tied the game at 5:43. More impressive was the play Heatley made to set up the go-ahead goal, by captain Daniel Alfredsson. Heatley swept at the puck as he was falling, and it landed on the stick of Alfredsson in the slot. He turned and fired in one motion, beating Tim Thomas. Patrick Eaves and Peter Schaefer added late goals to wrap up the win. It was Boston rookie Phil Kessel's first game back in the NHL after leaving the team several weeks earlier with testicular cancer. His was an inspiring return, but on this night not enough to stop the ever-expanding Ottawa juggernaut.

Game 46

January 11, 2007
Ottawa 6 at NY Rangers 4

The Ottawa Senators played for 43 minutes like the game was as easy as pie. They ended the game sweating bullets, squeaking out a victory that was way closer than they would have liked. By the first minute of the third period, they had built a huge 5-0 lead at Madison Square Garden, but then they allowed the Rangers to gain momentum and had to settle for an empty-net goal to show a two-goal differential on the scoresheet. Ottawa now boasted an 8-1-1 record in its past ten games, but after the game the players talked about a near disaster finish. Patrick Eaves scored the only goal of the first period to give Ottawa a slim 1-0 lead, but the Senators exploded for three more goals in the second. Chris Kelly and Antoine Vermette scored in the first two minutes, and Eaves made it 4-0 at 12:30. The Sens were in control and the Rangers were falling apart. Coach Tom Renney pulled Kevin Weekes in favour of Henrik Lundqvist, but that had little effect right away. Daniel

Alfredsson scored at 1:02 of the third to make it 5-0, and the team seemed on its way to an emphatic win. Such was the atmosphere in the building that when the Rangers' own Petr Prucha scored at 3:29, the New York crowd jeered in mock derision. When Jason Ward scored a minute later, they cheered with a modicum of effort, and when Marcel Hossa made it 5-3 at 6:10 they cheered full volume, knowing they now had a game on their hands. Blair Betts made it an uncomfortable 5-4 midway through the period, but that was as close as the Rangers got. Ottawa hung on and Dany Heatley scored into the empty net to make it 6-4. A win, to be sure, but not how the Senators had envisioned it when it was 5-0 early in the third period.

Jaromir Jagr of the Rangers tries to come out front on a wraparound, but goalie Ray Emery is there, waiting.

Game 47

January 13, 2007
Montreal 3 at Ottawa 8

This afternoon game kicked off *Hockey Day in Canada* in which all Canadian teams played each other, but it kicked off with a mighty bang for Ottawa and an embarrassing whimper for the Habs. If anything, the score flattered Montreal as Ottawa scored early, often, and seemingly at will. Captain Daniel Alfredsson led the romp with a goal and four assists. In all, eight different players scored for the Sens. Ottawa was 9-1-1 in its last eleven games and was now just a single point behind Montreal for second place in the Northeast Division. Ottawa scored four times in the first and four more in the second. By the 24th minute the Sens were up 6-0, and a brief rally by Montreal in which Chris Higgins and Craig Rivet scored just 22 seconds apart woke up the Sens to the possibility of another rally as they had allowed against the Rangers two nights earlier. They responded with two more goals. Two of their four goals in the first came on the power play, and on the day they were three-for-five with the man advantage. After Chris Kelly made it 6-0, Montreal coach Guy Carbonneau replaced goalie Cristobal Huet with David Aebischer. Dany Heatley scored his 28th goal of the year. Improbably, Montreal outshot Ottawa 40-33, but many shots were routine saves for Ray Emery while Montreal had pucks bounce in from funny places and every conceivable angle.

Game 48

January 16, 2007
Washington 2 at Ottawa 5

The Senators reeled off their fifth straight win, a season high, and moved into fourth place in the Eastern Conference with 56 points after defeating Washington. Here was another high-scoring effort, this time at the expense of the falling Capitals. Mike Comrie had two goals for Ottawa, bringing to four his total since joining Ottawa seven games ago. The teams combined for three goals in the first period, all in the final three minutes. Andrej Meszaros scored at 16:56 and Comrie got his first of the night on the power play when goalie Brent Johnson knocked the puck toward his own net and the Senators forward was there to finish the play off. Dany Heatley deserved some credit for helping to knock the puck free from the goalie's equipment. Chris Clark made it 2-1 with a short-handed goal with just 2.3 seconds left in the period. The Senators came out to start the second period with a poise that is learned through experience. Rather than let Washington gain momentum from that late goal, it was the Sens who counted the only two scores of the middle 20 minutes. Daniel Alfredsson scored short-handed and Comrie got his second of the game. Alfredsson's proved to be the game winner, his fourth such goal in a row. Steve Eminger tried to ignite a Capitals rally early in the third when he made it a 4-2 game, but Peter Schaefer restored the three-goal cushion a few minutes later to hand the Caps their third straight loss. Most important, the Sens prevented Alexander Ovechkin from being a factor, limiting his shots to those from long range or bad angle.

Chris Phillips got the first goal of the game against Boston's Hannu Toivonen. It proved to be the game winner.

Game 49

January 18, 2007
Vancouver 2 at **Ottawa 1**

The Senators lost to Vancouver and Montreal won its game, allowing the Habs to sneak back into fourth place in the Eastern Conference on a night Ottawa played well enough to win. As everyone in the building acknowledged, the difference was Vancouver goalie Roberto Luongo who stopped 34 of 35 shots. In the third period alone, Ottawa held a 14-0 shots advantage and limited the Canucks to just 14 shots all game against Ray Emery, yet the team could do little to beat the hottest goalie in the league. Vancouver had now won ten of its last eleven games. The first period was scoreless and the Canucks scored the only two goals of the second period. Both Taylor Pyatt and Rory Fitzpatrick scored by deflections, leaving Emery little chance to make the save on either play. The third period was as impressive a one as Ottawa had played all year. The team tied an NHL record by preventing even a single Vancouver shot all period, and the Sens made it a 2-1 game midway through on a Daniel Alfredsson goal via a great pass from Dany Heatley. Heatley later hit the crossbar on a breakaway, which was indicative of how the night was playing out for the two teams. Despite an all-out attack and two power-play chances, though, Ottawa couldn't tie the score. Emery left the net in the final minute for a sixth attacker, but that had no bearing on the game's outcome.

Game 50

January 20, 2007
Ottawa 3 at **Boston 0**

The Senators went into the mid-week All-Star Game break on a high note, shutting out Boston by scoring once late in each period. Ray Emery earned his fourth shutout of the year, and his Sens more than doubled the shot count on the home team, 39-18. It was an excellent effort in every aspect of the game for the Senators. Chris Phillips got the first goal of the game when his long shot caromed off a Boston player past goalie Hannu Toivonen at 17:16. In the second, it was a Dany Heatley power-play goal that made it 2-0. Tom Preissing's point shot was stopped by Toivonen but the puck fell to the ice where Heatley scooped up the rebound. Heatley added his 30th goal of the year into the empty net late in the third. Ottawa had a great chance to blow the game open late in the second. Boston enforcer Andrew Alberts hammered Chris Kelly from behind along the boards and received a five-minute major and game misconduct, and Marc Savard was given a minor penalty on the same play. But Ottawa couldn't score on the two-minute five-on-three opportunity and took a penalty early in the third to dim the effect of the lengthy power play. The fracas was payback for a hit earlier in the period when Christoph Schubert received a five-minute boarding major. The Senators now had a full week off before their next game, another match against these same Bruins on the other side of the all-star festivities in Dallas, Texas.

2007 All-Star Game

Dany Heatley (right, wearing number 16) hugs Daniel Briere (left, number 48) and Marian Hossa after combining for a goal during the 2007 All-Star Game in Dallas. Heatley was the lone Ottawa Senators representative at the game, although Andrej Meszaros took part in the Young Stars Game the previous day.

Antoine Vermette jumps to avoid a shot as goalie Tim Thomas makes the save.

Game 51

January 27, 2007
Boston 1 at **Ottawa** 3

The Senators came out of the All-Star break as they went into it—by beating Boston. This was a more convincing win at home before a raucous crowd of 19,846 at Scotiabank Place. The game was scoreless for two periods, but the Senators broke free in the final 20 minutes to take the two points. It was the first game back for Jason Spezza who missed five weeks with a knee injury. He contributed an assist on the first goal of the game, by Patrick Eaves early in the third. Eaves got the puck in the slot with his back to the net, but he spun quickly and fired, beating Tim Thomas between the legs. The Senators made it 2-0 five minutes later thanks to Chris Neil. He took a Peter Schaefer pass and blasted the puck over Thomas's glove. Glen Murray drew the Bruins within a goal a minute later, ending Ray Emery's shutout sequence at 135:44 minutes. They Bruins never threatened after that, though, and Ottawa went on to win. Boston's best chance to get closer came in the final minute when Chris Kelly took a hooking penalty at 18:57. With Thomas on the bench to create a two-man advantage, though, Antoine Vermette stole the puck and went in alone on the empty net. Marc Savard threw his stick to prevent the goal, so referee Kevin Pollock had no choice but to award Vermette the goal. Emery stopped 29 of 30 shots for the Sens.

Game 52

January 29, 2007
Ottawa 1 at **Montreal** 3

On the night the Canadiens honoured goalie great Ken Dryden, current Habs netminder David Aebischer had a start to the game he wanted to forget. In pre-game ceremonies that lasted well over an hour, Montreal retired Dryden's number 29, but in the first minute of play Aebischer watched a long Chris Phillips shot sail over his shoulder and into the net to silence the celebrating crowd. Fortunately for the Bell Centre faithful, this was the only thing that went wrong all night. The Habs played patient hockey and the Sens failed to increase their lead. Montreal scored three unanswered goals in less than three minutes in the second period to win. The two points moved the team one ahead of Ottawa in the Eastern Conference standings. Sheldon Souray tied the game for Montreal doing what he does best—driving a hard slapshot from the point on the power play. His shot beat Ray Emery cleanly. Emery was starting his eighth straight game for Ottawa. Just over a minute later, Montreal took the lead when Mark Streit scored on a breakaway courtesy of a great pass from Andrei Markov in his own end. The Swiss player, who converted to a winger from defenceman at the behest of coach Guy Carbonneau, looked like a veteran sniper with his slight fake and touch shot between Emery's pads as the goalie committed to the deke. If that wasn't enough, Tomas Plekanec scored short-handed just 78 seconds later, the team's league-leading 13th goal while down a man. The rest of the game was quiet and uneventful, and Ottawa headed home to regroup for a game less than 24 hours later against the Capitals.

Washington's sensational Alexander Semin tries to knock the puck out of mid-air, but Martin Gerber is there to block the shot.

Game 53

January 30, 2007
Washington 2 at Ottawa 3

As the previous night, the Senators jumped into the early lead, but this night they increased the lead and won in convincing fashion on Canadian Forces Appreciation Night. Some 1,500 Canadian soldiers were among the 19,178 fans at Scotiabank Place, and they witnessed a night of fast-paced action and great skill. Daniel Alfredsson scored at 9:51 of the first period to stake Ottawa to a 1-0 lead. His point shot eluded a number of bodies in front of Olaf Kolzig and found the back of the net behind the screened goalie. Jason Spezza made it 2-0 before the end of the period, scoring his 20th of the season and first since returning three games ago from a knee injury. He picked up a loose puck and found the open side of the net before Kolzig could come across to block that part of the goal. Alexander Ovechkin got his Capitals back in the game midway through the second, scoring his league-leading 32nd goal during a four-on-four situation. Not to be outdone, though, Dany Heatley replied a minute and a half later to restore Ottawa's comfortable two-goal cushion, and only a Donald Brashear goal in the third got past Martin Gerber the rest of the night. Gerber had been playing infrequently in the last three months and yet, paradoxically, had a 5-1 record in a relief role. Ray Emery had clearly become the starter, but Gerber's play as backup was encouraging for the Sens. The win allowed Ottawa to reclaim fourth place in the conference standings as Montreal did not play this night.

Game 54

February 3, 2007
Toronto 3 at Ottawa 2 (SO)

Ottawa's latest shootout experience of the 2006-07 season was a bad one as John Pohl of the Leafs scored on the ninth shot of the extra-point competition to give Toronto the win at Scotiabank Place. Only one of five Ottawa shots beat goalie Andrew Raycroft as the Battle of Ontario closed another chapter with a dramatic finish. It was a game either team could rightly claim deserved to win in regulation. Both teams played one period evenly, dominated a period, and were shelled in a period. A goalless opening 20 minutes gave way to a fierce Toronto offensive barrage in the second. The Leafs outshot Ottawa 18-8 and scored the only two goals, heading to the dressing room after 40 minutes seemingly in control. Jeff O'Neill opened the scoring thanks to a great pass by Matt Stajan on a two-on-one, and captain Mats Sundin made it 2-0 at 14:52. Ottawa coach Bryan Murray tore a strip off his players during the break, and it was the Sens who came out flying in the third. Sundin's counterpart, Ottawa/Swedish captain Daniel Alfredsson, got the Sens on the board at 4:47 and then Mike Comrie tied the game three and a half minutes later. Defenceman Joe Corvo had the puck behind his own net and spotted Comrie streaking up ice. He hit him with a perfect pass, and Comrie made no mistake on the breakaway. The shootout was a different story. Antoine Vermette gave Ottawa a 1-0 lead after the first pair of shooters, but Comrie, Mike Fisher, Dany Heatley, and Jason Spezza all failed to beat Raycroft. Pohl's nice deke gave Toronto the advantage, and after Spezza missed the game was over.

Patrick Eaves lugs the puck up ice against the Sabres.

Game 55

February 7, 2007
Ottawa 2 at Buffalo 3

Playing for the first time in four days, Ottawa showed plenty of life but not enough finish. The result was a second straight loss thanks to a late goal in the third period from Thomas Vanek, his second of the night. Buffalo, on the other hand, had played the previous night in Atlanta, proving that rest sometimes isn't all it's cracked up to be. Vanek opened the scoring midway through the second period by producing a goalscorer's goal. He picked off a pass by Anton Volchenkov and went in alone on Ray Emery at an angle, but instead of shooting or deking he held onto the puck and calmly went behind the net. Emery committed himself, and Vanek came out the other side to put the puck in the open net. Dean McAmmond replied for Ottawa just 41 seconds later, though. He picked up a loose puck near Martin Biron after the goalie had stopped Joe Corvo, and he whacked it home for his first goal in 14 games to make it 1-1. Maxim Afinogenov restored Buffalo's lead before the end of the second when his hard shot went off the post and in. Peter Schaefer tied the game again early in the third. Ottawa had a lengthy five-on-three which went for naught, but just as the second penalty was about to end he corralled a loose puck off an Andrej Meszaros point shot and ripped it past Biron from close range. Vanek's game winner came at 16:00 on the power play. He had one shot from in close that Emery stopped, but in the ensuing scramble the puck came back to him with the goalie out of position and he lifted it home. Ottawa could not mount any sustained attack in the dying minutes.

Game 56

February 8, 2007
Montreal 1 at Ottawa 4

Ottawa ended its two-game losing streak with an impressive win over Montreal to move once again one point ahead of the Canadiens in the standings. The team was powered by its big stars and a rash of Montreal penalties. Coach Bryan Murray also put his top scorers—Jason Spezza and Dany Heatley—together again for the first time since before Spezza's pre-Christmas injury. Each scored tonight. Ottawa had the only goal of the first period, thanks to Chris Phillips. His long shot was caught by goalie Cristobal Huet, but the puck popped out of his glove and trickled over the goal line. Heatley made it 2-0 in the first minute of the second period after a great pass from Spezza. He found his teammate open in front, and Heatley made no mistake with the quick shot to record his 32nd goal of the season. Peter Schaefer's power-play goal late in the period made it a solid 3-0 score, and Montreal scored its only goal a short time later. Guillaume Latendresse was high-sticked by Phillips on a breakaway, and the Montreal rookie was awarded his first career penalty shot by referee Rob Shick. Phillips was also penalized on the play. Latendresse made no mistake with the free shot, but Montreal failed to convert the man advantage situation. In all, Montreal was goalless in six power plays while handing Ottawa eight man advantage opportunities, including three in a row during one brief stretch of the middle period. Spezza scored the game's final goal with less than two minutes to play on a four-on-three rush.

Game 57

February 10, 2007
Ottawa 5 at Montreal 3

Ottawa completed a home-and-home sweep by beating the Canadiens in Montreal, but the Sens had a tougher time of it at the Bell Centre than at Scotiabank Place a day earlier. The Senators built an impressive 2-0 lead in the first only to see the Habs tie the game by the midway point of the second period. They then put their game into overdrive, scored three in a row, and went on to win. The game featured a controversial play in the Ottawa crease when goalie Ray Emery slashed Montreal forward Maxim Lapierre in the face. Although all parties admitted afterward it was a violent play, Emery defended himself by saying he was frustrated by the amount of crease-crashing the referees had permitted in his blue ice. Emery snapped, and although he earned only a minor penalty on the play he was later suspended by the league for three games. The Sens struck first just 2:10 into the game on a Mike Comrie goal. Chris Kelly made it 2-0 midway through the period and the Habs were looking lost. They got back into the game in the second after an Emery error behind his net. He fumbled the puck and Mike Johnson got it out front to Steve Begin who had the open net to shoot at. Michael Ryder tied the game on the power play while Mike Comrie was in the box serving Emery's penalty, but after that play the goalie settled down while his counterpart, David Aebischer, looked weak at best. Wade Redden gave the Sens the lead again late in the second, and Mike Fisher and Jason Spezza put the game out of reach with early goals in the third. Montreal held a 40-30 advantage in shots, but goaltending proved the difference. The Razor's edge proved sharper than the bad Hab-its Aebischer brought to the Montreal crease this night.

Without use of his stick, Ray Emery makes a diving, lunging save while Montreal's Mike Johnson looks for the loose puck.

Game 58

February 14, 2007
Florida 0 at **Ottawa 4**

Filling in for the suspended Ray Emery, Martin Gerber stopped all 29 shots to lead the Sens to a convincing 4-0 win over Florida. It was his first shutout in more than 13 months. Four different players scored for Ottawa. The win kept the team in a tie for fourth place with Pittsburgh in the Eastern Conference. Chris Phillips opened the scoring at 8:21 of the first. He took the puck behind the Florida net, came out in front, and as goalie Ed Belfour went down to cover the wraparound, Phillips shot high. Mike Fisher made it 2-0 in the second period thanks to a defensive error by the Panthers. Ruslan Salei was checked off the puck behind his own goal by Peter Schaefer, and he quickly passed out front to Fisher who one-timed it past a surprised Belfour. The Sens got their final two goals in the third period. Mike Comrie scored on a five-on-three and Dean McAmmond made it 4-0 a few minutes later. Although shots were 33-28 for Ottawa, the Panthers had few real scoring chances and were never a threat this night. Had Gerber needed to be replaced in goal, coach Bryan Murray would have inserted backup Kelly Guard who had been called up from Binghamton but had yet to play a minute in the NHL.

Mike Comrie scores on Atlanta's Kari Lehtonen in the third period to tie the game, 3-3, and spark an Ottawa rally for victory.

Game 59

February 17, 2007
Atlanta 3 at Ottawa 5

The Senators won their fourth in a row, earning two points at Scotiabank Place by coming from behind after trailing heading into the third period. The Sens scored the only three goals of the final 20 minutes to cap a last-period rally for only the third time this season. The nosediving Thrashers had now won only once in the last eight games. Martin Gerber started for the second game while Ray Emery was serving his three-game suspension, and he stopped 28 of 31 shots for the win. Kari Lehtonen was the losing goalie. The Thrashers scored first on a Steve McCarthy power-play goal at 11:00. His screen shot went past Gerber without the goalie moving. Peter Schaefer evened the score in the final minute when he scooped up a loose puck and knocked it in, but Atlanta made two of the three goals in the second period. Glen Metropolit scored early to make it 2-1 for the Thrashers, and Chris Kelly scored short-handed three minutes later after Lehtonen gave up a generous rebound off a routine shot from Antoine Vermette. Slava Kozlov gave the Thrashers their third lead of the game in the final minute while on the power play, but it was all Ottawa in the third period. Mike Comrie tied the game at 10:05. Dean McAmmond, playing on the number-one line with Jason Spezza and Dany Heatley, gave the Sens their first lead when he converted a Spezza pass in front. Mike Fisher then assured victory with a last-minute goal. Spezza was the target of hulking Atlanta defenceman Andy Sutton all night and handled himself well. Sutton took one penalty on the night, and Spezza chipped in two assists.

Game 60

February 20, 2007
Edmonton 3 at Ottawa 4

Ottawa won a shootout for the first time this season and in the process put coach Bryan Murray in the history books. Murray became just the fifth man to win 600 career games behind the bench (after Scotty Bowman, Al Arbour, Dick Irvin, and Pat Quinn). He can thank shootout scorers Dean McAmmond and Mike Comrie and goalie Martin Gerber for gaining the historic win. Besides that, it was, at best, an unorthodox win for Ottawa, as the team blew a 3-1 lead late in the third period. In fact, the Senators were in full control after 40 minutes. Dany Heatley scored in the first and Mike Fisher in the second to give them a solid 2-0 lead, and they were playing a solid defensive game as well. Nothing suggested the third-period collapse that ensued. Heatley beat Jussi Markkanen with a low shot and Fisher went high over the glove for his goal. Petr Sykora got Edmonton on the board just 1:34 into the final period on a power play, but Daniel Alfredsson made it 3-1 at 12:17. His was a classic. He took a pass in full stride, burst through the defence, and beat Markkanen with a beautiful move for the goal. Then disaster struck. Sykora scored again at 15:48 off a turnover by Chris Kelly, and rookie Tom Gilbert scored his first career goal with Markkanen on the bench and just 19.9 seconds left in regulation time. Both teams had good chances to score in the overtime, but it was the shootout that decided the game. Martin Gerber stopped Ales Hemsky and Sykora while McAmmond and Comrie made good on Markkanen. It was Ottawa's fifth straight win and lowered Edmonton's current road trip record to 0-3-1.

Game 61

February 22, 2007
Ottawa 5 at Buffalo 6 (SO)

Buffalo's Tomas Vanek makes a great deflection to score on Ray Emery in Buffalo's 6-5 win at HSBC Arena.

In one of the maddest, wildest games of the year, Ottawa lost in a shootout. But that wasn't the talk of the town after the game. No, the talk centred around a series of events in the second period. Five minutes in, Chris Neil of Ottawa nearly decapitated Buffalo's top player, Chris Drury, with a hit that sent Drury to the hospital and left a small pool of blood on the ice. The Sens claimed the severity of the hit was the result of Drury having his head down while handling the puck; the Sabres said the hit was a dirty and vicious elbow worthy of a game misconduct and suspension. No penalty was called, but Neil fought with Drew Stafford after the hit. On the next shift, Buffalo coach Lindy Ruff sent out three fighters against Ottawa's top-scoring line, and an all-out melee ensued. Even goalies Ray Emery and Martin Biron got in on the action, and when they were done Buffalo goon Andrew Peters went after Emery. The coaches then exchanged angry words from their respective benches as the temperature rose further. In all, 17 penalties were called from this one brawl alone, and both goalies were given game misconducts, leaving their backups to decide the outcome. The emotions from the hit, from the playoff races, and from this growing rivalry, were palatable. As for the game, Ottawa lost a great opportunity to extend its winning streak to six. Emery was playing in his first game after serving a three-game suspension, but his night was cut short and Martin Gerber came in and allowed two goals plus the shootout winner. Ottawa took an early 2-0 lead on goals from Daniel Alfredsson and Dany Heatley, but the Sabres rattled off three in a row to take the lead. Heatley's second tied the game midway through the second period, and then each team scored two more goals in a row, first Buffalo, then Ottawa. Drew Stafford scored the only goal of eight shots in the shootout.

Game 62

February 24, 2007
Buffalo 5 at Ottawa 6

Same score, different winner, softer emotions. That's how tonight's rematch went after the wild brawl two days previous in Buffalo. The other main difference was that Jason Spezza provided the heroics with a power-play goal late in the third period, so no shootout was necessary as was the case in Buffalo. The heroics wouldn't have been necessary had the Sens not wasted a 4-1 lead which they had carefully built through the first half of the game. Henrik Tallinder scored first, at 2:27, when his shot from the point made it through bodies in front and beat the screened Ray Emery. Ottawa then reeled off four goals in a row, one later in the first and three early in the second in a span of 1:51. Jason Spezza scored short-handed to tie the game, and then Dany Heatley scored his 36th of the year at 6:12 of the second on the power play. Christoph Schubert and Chris Kelly also scored soon after to make it 4-1. But a Lindy Ruff team never quits, and the Sabres clawed back into the game. Thomas Vanek missed a penalty shot, but Derek Roy scored before the end of the period. Jason Pominville made it 4-3 just 38 seconds into the third. Daniel Alfredsson made it 5-3, but Buffalo scored twice to tie the game. That set the stage for Spezza. Teppo Numminen was called for interference at 15:46, and off the next faceoff Heatley stole the puck from goalie Ryan Miller behind the Buffalo net and passed out front to Spezza who scored on the empty net. It was a hard-fought, playoff-style win for the Senators, a true character builder, as they say.

Ottawa's Anton Volchenkov collides with Carolina's Andrew Ladd behind the Sens' net.

Game 63

February 27, 2007
Ottawa 4 at Carolina 2

The Senators played come-from-behind hockey again, taking the early lead, giving it up, and rallying for their seventh win in the last eight games. It came at the expense of a faltering Hurricanes team that was looking less and less like Stanley Cup champions with the passing of every week. On this night, they had a 2-1 lead after 40 minutes, but Ottawa pulled away, scoring the only three goals of the third. Dany Heatley opened the scoring at 5:08 of the second period when he scooped a rebound past John Grahame in net, his 37th goal of the season. The Sens then had a brief but costly collapse a few minutes later, allowing two Carolina goals in 19 seconds. Eric Staal and Josef Vasicek did the damage. The Sens outshot the Hurricanes 15-8 in the final period and took complete control of the game. Anton Volchenkov hammered a Chris Phillips pass over the shoulder of Grahame to tie the score at 10:49. It was the first goal in more than a year for the defenceman. Four and a half minutes later, Jason Spezza carried the puck down the left side and waited patiently for something to develop. He was at the goal line before he saw the play he wanted, and at that moment defenceman Chris Phillips jumped into the rush and headed for the goal. Spezza fired a hard pass, Phillips got good wood on the redirect, and the Senators had a 3-2 lead. Spezza himself finished the scoring with an empty netter in the final minute. Coach Bryan Murray again started former 'Canes goalie Martin Gerber, and the plan worked as well as it had earlier in the season.

Game 64

February 28, 2007
Carolina 0 at **Ottawa 2**

Ray Emery was back in goal despite Martin Gerber's success against his old club, but that didn't matter much. Emery blocked all 27 shots to earn his fifth shutout of the season and give Ottawa consecutive wins against Carolina in this home-and-home series. It improved the Sens' record to 8-0-1 in the past nine games. Jason Spezza had a goal and an assist, and Ottawa's penalty killing did yeomen's work, notably in the third period when the team incurred five of six minors and played short-handed for nearly eight minutes. Dany Heatley scored the opening goal just 3:54 into the first period. Spezza fought to get to a loose puck behind the Carolina goal and threw it out front. Heatley controlled the puck, spun to his forehand, and beat Cam Ward low to the glove side. The Senators nursed this lead for the next 40 minutes until Spezza made it 2-0 off a counter attack. Playing four-on-three, Carolina came in over the Ottawa blueline only to have Andrej Meszaros break up the play. He made a quick pass to defence partner Chris

Phillips who saw Spezza leave the penalty box in the same moment. Phillips hit him flying up the middle with a breakaway pass. Spezza made no mistake, roofing a wrist shot that beat Ward cleanly. Coach Bryan Murray had Heatley and Spezza back together with Daniel Alfredsson as he chose to place all his top scoring eggs in one basket, as it were.

Game 65
March 2, 2007
Ottawa 2 at **Atlanta 4**

As Slava Kozlov goes, so goes Atlanta's chances of beating Ottawa. For the third time this year, it was Kozlov who scored the winning goal against the Senators. He had 15 goals on the year now—seven of which he registered against Ottawa. For the Sens, the loss was tough to swallow because they blew a lead after two periods and watched the Thrashers score the only three goals of the final period. Dany Heatley had both Ottawa goals including his 40th of the season. The teams traded first-period goals. Eric Belanger got the game's first score midway through the period courtesy of a Jason Spezza giveaway. His dangerous pass through the middle in his own end didn't get to his target as Belanger stepped in front, stole the puck, and ripped a wrist shot past Ray Emery. Heatley replied a few minutes later on the power play. His bad-angle shot squeezed through the pads of Kari Lehtonen, a shot the goalie should have handled. The Senators controlled play in the second period but could manage only one goal. Heatley again scored on a power-play shot, but this was a legitimate bullet that Lehtonen couldn't be faulted for missing. Belanger struck again, early in the third, to tie the game for the Thrashers. He took a long pass from Andy Sutton, ploughed past defenceman Andrej Meszaros, and beat Emery with a nice move. Kozlov scored the go-ahead goal thanks to ex-Senators Marian Hossa. He fought off two Ottawa defenceman and got the puck out front, and Kozlov's seeing-eye shot found the back of the net through a group of players in front. Pascal Dupuis put the game out of reach at 15:04.

Daniel Alfredsson scores the go-ahead goal in Chicago during a 4-3 shootout loss to the Hawks.

Game 66
March 4, 2007
Ottawa 3 at **Chicago 4** (SO)

The Senators lost their second straight road game, this in Chicago via a shootout. Again, they blew a third-period lead, but this loss hurt all the more because Chicago had long been playing in the shadows of playoff-bound teams. Radim Vrbata was the hero for the Hawks, scoring twice in regulation and adding the shootout winner for good measure. He got the game's first goal at 6:24 on a nice give-and-go with former Sens forward Martin Havlat that finished with Vrbata making a nice deflection of Havlat's shot. Newly-acquired Oleg Saprykin tied it for Ottawa when he collected his own rebound and beat former Senators goalie Patrick Lalime with a quick shot, his first goal in a Senators sweater. Ottawa outshot the Hawks 12-6 in the second and scored twice to take a 3-1 lead to the third. Daniel Alfredsson scored on a power play off a rebound, finishing off a Dany Heatley shot that Lalime blocked. Then, Antoine Vermette deftly redirected Andrej Meszaros's shot for the two-goal lead. The final period belonged to Chicago. Mikael Holmqvist made it 3-2 with a wrist shot from in close and then Vrbata tied the game with just 1:59 left in regulation while the teams were playing four-on-four. In the shootout, the first four skaters failed to score. Heatley put the pressure on by scoring on Ottawa's final attempt, but Jeff Hamilton calmly made a great deke and backhand to tie the score. Vermette missed for Ottawa and Vrbata made a similar move to Hamilton's to win it for the Hawks.

Sidney Crosby goes high on the backhand to beat Ray Emery to give Pittsburgh the shootout win.

Game 67

March 6, 2007
Pittsburgh 5 at Ottawa 4 (SO)

Every team loses. There's no doubting that. But there are losses and there are losses, and tonight the Senators really, really lost one. In complete control and ahead 4-1 after two periods, the Sens allowed the Penguins to tie the game in regulation and then, thanks to Sid the Kid, lost the game and a valuable extra point, in the shootout. It was Ottawa's third straight defeat. Sidney Crosby was held without a point during the 65 minutes of playing time, but his young teammates proved adept at scoring in his absence. Colby Armstrong got the Pens on the scoreboard first, but Ottawa took advantage of a weak night from Marc-Andre Fleury to score three times before the end of the period. Mike Fisher, Christoph Schubert, and Chris Kelly did the damage for the Senators. The last was especially damaging for the Pens as it came off a weak shot from outside the blueline. Coach Michel Therrien pulled Fleury in favour of Jocelyn Thibault, and the Penguins settled down. Still, it was the Sens who got the only goal of the second to increase their lead to a comfortable 4-1, Dany Heatley getting the goal on the power play, his 41st of the year. But Pittsburgh, young and talented, knew no fear and came out in the third willing to lose 10-1 if it gave them a chance to get back in the game. Jordan Staal brought the team a bit closer with a great short-handed goal, his league-best seventh of the year on a great shot over Emery's glove, and a minute and a half later newcomer Gary Roberts made his contribution with a goal to make it 5-4. Ryan Malone completed the comeback just 68 seconds after Roberts, and that's how the game ended after 60 minutes. Shots were 11-2 Penguins in the final period. In the shootout, Erik Christensen scored on Pittsburgh's first shot. Dean McAmmond tied the game with Ottawa's final shot, leaving the game in the hands of Crosby or Ray Emery. Crosby got the better of the goalie by roofing a backhander to send the Sens to the dressing room more than a little upset with their performance this night.

Game 68

March 8, 2007
Toronto 1 at **Ottawa 5**

The Senators were not about to blow another third-period lead. So, when they were up 4-1 after two periods, they kept pushing once the third got under way. They scored early in the final period, and then played solid defensive hockey to ensure there would be no rally by the opposition, least of all the loathed Maple Leafs. Daniel Alfredsson played perhaps his best game of the year, contributing three assists in the win to snap a three-game losing streak, each loss the result of a late blown lead. The Sens scored the only two goals of the first and added a third early in the middle period to make it a 3-0 game. They outshot the Leafs by a whopping 23-7 margin in the opening 20 minutes. Both goals came off the stick of Mike Fisher, and both came with the extra man as Ottawa capitalized on its first two power-play chances. Alfredsson assisted on both goals and added his third helper on Dean McAmmond's short-handed goal at 3:51 of the second. Alexander Steen scored for Toronto on a nice rush to make it 3-1 halfway through the game, but that was all the fight the Leafs could offer up this night. Tom Preissing scored late on the power play and McAmmond added his second of the game early in the final period to give the Sens a comfortable lead against a struggling opponent. Heatley extended his point-scoring streak to 13 games by getting an assist on McAmmond's third-period goal.

Game 69

March 10, 2007
Ottawa 3 at Toronto 4 (OT)

Ottawa was back in trouble with its confidence again after blowing another solid lead in the third period, this time allowing the Leafs to fight from 3-1 down to send the game into overtime. Darcy Tucker scored the winner at 3:11 of the extra period for the Leafs, leaving the Senators reeling from their apparent inability to finish what they frequently started so well. The Senators scored the only goal of the first and added a second goal early in the middle period to build an impressive 2-0 lead over the Leafs, who lost badly to Ottawa two nights ago despite being in a desperate battle for the final playoff spot in the Eastern Conference. Daniel Alfredsson had a hand in both goals, scoring the first off a rebound and teeing the puck up for a Mike Fisher one-timer on the power play on the second one. Tucker got his first of the night on a patented pass from Mats Sundin on the power play. Sundin, stationed near the red line to Ray Emery's stick side, drilled a hard pass through the crease and Tucker banged it home to the back side. Dany Heatley scored what should have been the back-breaker, a last-minute goal in the second period while playing short-handed. But the Leafs were the better team in the final period and tied the game with two goals, one from Boyd Devereaux, the other from Nik Antropov at 15:58. Tucker's winner came after a great bit of stick-handling and set-up from Matt Stajan. After the first period, the Leafs outshot Ottawa 31-11 and were the more desperate team. Were it not for the great play of Emery in Ottawa's goal, Toronto wouldn't have needed extra time to win this one.

Jason Spezza tucks the puck expertly between the pads of Henrik Lundqvist of the Rangers to score Ottawa's first goal of the game and ignite a comeback win.

Game 70

March 13, 2007
Ottawa 3 at NY Rangers 2

Reversing their fortunes of recent games, Ottawa overcame a slow start and a 2-0 deficit to rally for the win at Madison Square Garden. Andrej Meszaros's pinball special midway through the third period proved to be the game-winning goal this night. Michael Nylander scored both Rangers' goals in the first period, but Jason Spezza started the comeback midway through the second period. His goal came at the exact time Paul Mara came out of the penalty box to make it 2-1 (oddly, the NHL does not consider it a power-play goal if a goal is scored exactly two minutes after the penalty time). Spezza scooped up a rebound after Henrik Lundqvist made the save off a Chris Phillips shot but couldn't control the rebound. Daniel Alfredsson tied the game a few minutes later, this time just seven seconds after Mara had freed himself from the penalty box. These were the only penalties the Rangers incurred all night, but the damage was done. In the third, Spezza made a great play to set up Meszaros for the winning score. He dragged the puck down the right side waiting for help, saw the defenceman move into the high slot, and fed him a perfect pass through a maze of legs. Meszaros, in turn, saw Dany Heatley streak to the net and made a hard pass that was deflected by Rangers' defenceman Marek Malik right into the top corner of his own goal past a stunned Lundqvist. The Rangers did everything but tie the game, and it was up to Ray Emery to come up with the play of the game. He made a tremendous stop off a Martin Straka backhand from the top of the crease with 40 seconds left on the clock.

Wade Redden has a chance in close on Islanders' goalie Mike Dunham.

Game 71

March 15, 2007
NY Islanders 2 at Ottawa 5

Ottawa capitalized on a big break by scoring five goals to start the game, chasing backup goalie Mike Dunham who started the game because number-one goalie Rick DiPietro had suffered a neck injury in the Islanders' previous outing against Montreal. The Senators set a team record along the way, scoring three goals in just 76 seconds early in the third period. The win pushed Ottawa ahead of Pittsburgh for fourth place in the Eastern Conference with 89 points, one more than the Penguins, while the loss left the Islanders tied for seventh place with Carolina at 78 points. Ottawa was leading 5-0 four minutes into the third period. Both Islanders goals were scored late in the third with the game long out of reach. The first period was scoreless, but Chris Kelly and Joe Corvo got Ottawa started early in the second. The third period rampage featured goals by Chris Neil, Dean McAmmond, and Jason Spezza, and drove Dunham from the goal. He was replaced by popular minor leaguer Wade Dubielewicz who stopped all eight shots he faced. Miroslav Satan scored on a five-on-three with five minutes left in the game and Drew Fata made it 5-2 with 4.2 seconds left. Ray Emery stopped 28 of 30 shots in the victory. It was the seventh straight win by the Sens over the Islanders.

Game 72

March 17, 2007
Philadelphia 2 at Ottawa 3

Despite being far removed from the playoff race, the Flyers provided stiff opposition for Ottawa for this Saturday night game. It was a low-scoring contest marked by fine goaltending at either end, backup Martin Gerber in goal for Ottawa and Martin Biron in net for the Flyers. The result gave Ottawa four wins over Philadelphia in as many games this year. Mike Comrie snapped out of a recent slump with a goal and assist using a pink stick in the second annual Tribute to Hockey Moms event supported by hundreds of NHLers to make people more aware of breast cancer. Comrie's mother died of the disease when he was ten years old, so the cause was near to his heart. Comrie started the play that led to the first goal. His shot was stopped by Biron, but Tom Preissing whacked the rebound in for the early lead. The Flyers came right back, though, and tied the game just 66 seconds later. Mike Richards made a nice wraparound move that fooled Gerber. Comrie got the only goal of the second period—and his first in 13 games—thanks to some hard work behind the net. He won a battle with Mike York for the puck, stepped out in front, and beat Biron with a quick shot. Peter Schaefer made it 3-2 midway through the third and Derian Hatcher made it closer at 16:36, but the Flyers never had sustained pressure in the Ottawa end thereafter and were unable to tie the score.

Game 73

March 18, 2007
Ottawa 3 at Pittsburgh 4 (SO)

The Senators lost a hard-fought and emotional game with playoff implications. Jarkko Ruutu scored the decisive goal at the end of a shootout after the Sens had fought back three times from being down a goal. It was the second time in two weeks that the Penguins beat Ottawa via the penalty-shot format. The Penguins moved into a tie for fourth place with Ottawa as a result of the shootout win, making all the more possible an Ottawa-Pittsburgh date in the first round of the playoffs. It was Pittsburgh's fifth straight win. Maxime Talbot got the game's first goal while his team was playing short-handed. Three Penguins broke out on a rush, and Talbot finished it off with a shot that beat Ray Emery. Just 26 seconds later, however, Antoine Vermette tied the game for Ottawa. The pattern repeated itself in the second period. Sidney Crosby scored on a power play, but 61 seconds later Daniel Alfredsson deflected Joe Corvo's shot past Marc-Andre Fleury to make it 2-2. Ryan Whitney gave Pittsburgh its third lead later in the period, and it looked as though this time the lead would hold up. But with less than five minutes left in the game and Evgeni Malkin in the penalty box on a holding-the-stick call, Wade Redden let go a point shot that missed several bodies in front of the goalie and beat Fleury to tie the game. Overtime settled nothing, so it was back to the shootout for these teams. Ruutu scored on Pittsburgh's second shot, and all three Sens—Mike Comrie, Dean McAmmond, and Vermette—failed to light the lamp.

Game 74
March 20, 2007
Ottawa 4 at St. Louis 2

Ottawa defenceman Andrej Meszaros moves the puck along the boards, eluding Lee Stempniak of St. Louis along the way.

It wasn't the prettiest win or the most impressive, and the Senators got some help from the referees, but two points was added to the team's total in the standings after it was all over, and that's what mattered most. The Senators broke a 2-2 tie with the only two goals of the third period, and the Blues had two apparent goals disallowed at critical times of that same period. The first of those came early in the third with the game still tied. Brad Boyes scored, but Ottawa goalie Martin Gerber reached back and pulled the puck out before anyone could notice. Replays confirmed the goal, but play had already started so the goal could not be counted. Even referee Mick McGeough acknowledged to St. Louis coach Andy Murray the puck was in. A minute later, Antoine Vermette scored for Ottawa while Mike Fisher was in the penalty box, and just like that it was 3-2 Ottawa instead of 3-2 St. Louis. Then, with 2:18 left, David Backes figured he had scored, but Gerber again pulled the puck back. McGeough ruled this time that Gerber had made the save and was pushed back inside his goal after the whistle had sounded. Soon after, Chris Kelly scored into the empty net to make it a 4-2 game. St. Louis scored first on a Barret Jackman goal midway through the opening period. The Senators tied the game early in the second and took the lead at 12:39 when Fisher scored short-handed. He took the puck in centre ice, fought off a check, and blasted a shot past Curtis Sanford. Brad Boyes tied it late in the period to make it a 2-2 game after 40 minutes and set the table for Ottawa's rally in the third. It was Ottawa's first win in St. Louis since 1999 and the first time this year the team had scored two short-handed goals in a game.

Dean McAmmond makes a great shot to the far side of Tampa Bay's Karri Ramo for the goal during an Ottawa route of the Lightning.

Game 75
March 22, 2007
Ottawa 4 at Florida 2

Completing a four-game sweep of Florida this year, the Senators led 4-0 by the halfway point of the game, chased Panthers' goalie Ed Belfour from the crease, and cruised to their fifth victory in six games during their most recent streak of fine play. Dany Heatley led the way with his 43rd goal of the year while linemate Jason Spezza had a goal and an assist. Ray Emery stopped 35 of 37 Florida shots and was sharp on several occasions. Patrick Eaves scored at 2:31 of the first when his harmless-looking backhand beat Belfour over the glove. In the second period, Florida held a 14-4 advantage in shots but Ottawa scored on each of its first three, the last of which sent Belfour to the bench in favour of youngster Craig Anderson at 12:01. Jason Spezza made it 2-0 on the power play when he deflected Joe Corvo's shot to the top corner. Heatley made it 3-0 with another routine shot that Belfour muffed. Dean McAmmond made it 4-0 with a shot low to the stick side. Jozef Stumpel got one goal back for the Panthers before the end of the period, and Finnish captain Olli Jokinen cut the lead to 4-2 midway through the third with a tricky backhander. Florida could get no closer despite outshooting Ottawa by a wide margin, 37-19.

Game 76
March 24, 2007
Ottawa 7 at Tampa Bay 2

Firing on all cylinders, the Senators hammered Tampa Bay in a game Ottawa could say was good playoff preparation. Dany Heatley led the way with his 44th and 45th goals of the year plus one assist, and Ray Emery was strong in net, stopping 21 of 23 shots. Although the game was tied 2-2 early in the second period, the Senators kept pressing and soon enough the goals went rolling in, one after the other. In the end, it wasn't close. Joe Corvo set the tone with a goal just 2:38 into the game. He scored on a slapshot from the blueline that Marc Denis absolutely should have stopped. Dan Boyle got that one back on the power play later in the period, but Daniel Alfredsson gave the Sens a 2-1 lead just 53 seconds later when he made a nice deflection of a Heatley shot. Boyle scored again to tie the game 2-2, and after that it was all Ottawa all night. Heatley got his first at 12:41 of the second by tipping Joe Corvo's point shot on the power play, and 86 seconds later Christoph Schubert doubled the lead by beating Denis to the stick side with a one-timer off a Patrick Eaves set-up. Eaves's goal early in the third was enough for Tampa Bay coach John Tortorella, and he pulled Denis in favour of Finnish rookie Karri Ramo. Ramo surrendered the final two goals. All in all, the win bode well for Ottawa as it prepared for what it hoped would be a long post-season run.

Game 77
March 27, 2007
Boston 3 at Ottawa 2

Although Ottawa doubled the shot count on Boston, 34-17, Zdeno Chara proved the deadly poison against his old team again by scoring the winning goal in the third period. Boston ended a five-game losing streak as the Sens blew leads of 1-0 and 2-1. Dany Heatley scored his 46th of the year just 55 seconds after the opening faceoff, but Patrice Bergeron scored on the power play seven minutes later to tie the score. The period ended 1-1 only for a lack of finish by the Sens. They had five power-play opportunities in the opening 20 minutes but couldn't convert once. In the second, Ottawa again took the lead when Mike Fisher finally scored with the extra man. It was his 20th goal of the year. Two minutes later, though, Boston struck for a pair of quick goals. Peter Kalus scored his first of the year at 4:08, capitalizing on an Ottawa turnover in its own end, and just 37 seconds later Chara drove a hard point shot past Ray Emery. Ottawa outshot the Bruins 13-3 in the third, but Joey MacDonald was strong in the Boston goal and the Sens couldn't finish around the net. Lawrence Nycholat played his first game for Ottawa, replacing Wade Redden just before game time. The team now had three days off before its next game, a needed respite following its recent road trip.

Game 78

March 30, 2007
Montreal 2 at Ottawa 5

Mike Comrie tries to stuff the puck in but is denied by goalie Joey MacDonald.

Ottawa took a 3-1 lead to the dressing room after the first period and used the momentum to hand Montreal its first defeat in six games. For the Sens, the game was merely preparation for the playoffs, although it did give them an even 100 points in the standings. For the Habs, sitting in eighth place in the Eastern Conference, it was a huge loss. Dany Heatley scored his 47th goal of the year and Mike Comrie and Mike Fisher each had three-point nights. The game got off on the wrong foot for Montreal when rookie goalie Jaroslav Halak turned the puck over behind his own goal. His pass to a defenceman missed, and the Sens pounced on the error. Comrie got the puck to Peter Schaefer who moved it over to Fisher, and he made no mistake at 4:57 to give Ottawa the early lead. Jason Spezza made it 2-0 a minute and a half later, ripping a hard shot over the goalie's glove hand. Sheldon Souray got the Canadiens back in the game with another power play goal at 11:00 to make it 2-1. It was his 18th power-play goal, tying the NHL record for defencemen in a season. Comrie made it 3-1 late in the period, and then Montreal squandered a great opportunity to get back in the game. The Habs had a five-on-three for the full two minutes at the end of the first and start of the second, but the Sens hunkered down and killed the two concurrent penalties in impressive fashion. Despite a total of 29 shots being fired at Halak and Ray Emery in the middle period, there were no goals. Mark Streit made things interesting early in the third, and moments later he was robbed by a sensational glove save from Emery to keep it a 3-2 game. Fisher and Heatley scored later in the period to round out the goalscoring.

Mike Fisher flies over the back of Martin Brodeur.

Game 79

March 31, 2007
Ottawa 5 at NY Islanders 2

The battle of the backups was won by Ottawa this night, even though the number-two goalies were playing for radically different reasons. Martin Gerber was in net for Ottawa to give Ray Emery a break heading into the playoffs. Wade Dubielewicz was in goal for the Islanders, who were in the thick of a tough playoff fight, because Rick DiPietro was still suffering the effects of a concussion. Ottawa's firepower was no match for "Dubie," who was making his first start of the year. Dany Heatley scored his 48th goal of the season and Mike Comrie scored twice in the win. The loss left the Islanders still four points out of the playoffs with only four games remaining. Christoph Schubert got the only goal of the first, in the final minute, thanks to a great play by Jason Spezza. The pair roared up ice on a two-on-one, Spezza carrying the puck down the right wing. He timed the pass across perfectly, and all Schubert had to do was get his stick down and redirect the puck in the open side. The Isles got some life in the middle of the second when Viktor Kozlov tied the score, but just 28 seconds later Comrie got his first of the night. He deked Deron Quint out of his proverbial jock and then beat Dubielewicz with a great shot. The veteran Quint was signed by the Isles in desperation as they were looking for help on the blueline after a rash of injuries left them thin in that area. The Sens blew the game open with two quick goals in the third. Comrie and Dean McAmmond made it 4-1, and although Marc-Andre Bergeron scored on the power play later in the period for the Long Islanders, Ottawa remained in control. Heatley's goal came into the empty net. Ottawa outshot the Islanders, 47-23.

Game 80

April 3, 2007
Ottawa 1 at **New Jersey 2** (SO)

The storyline out of New Jersey rarely changes: few scoring chances, great goaltending from Martin Brodeur, and timely scoring. Tonight, the only additional news was that John Madden scored the shootout winner in the third extra round of the penalty-shot contest to give the Devils two points. The night was especially meaningful because Brodeur's win was his 47th of the year, tying the NHL record set by Bernie Parent of Philadelphia in 1973-74. For New Jersey, there was added motivation because general manager Lou Lamoriello was behind the bench one day after firing coach Claude Julien. For the longest time this looked like it might have been a scoreless game from start to finish. It wasn't until 10:15 of the third period that Madden opened the scoring by tipping a Brian Rafalski shot past Ray Emery. Just 21 seconds later, Daniel Alfredsson tied the game, working a nice passing play with Dany Heatley and making a nice shot to beat Brodeur. As if New Jersey was stung by this burst of offence, it made sure no further offensive damage would be done until the shootout. The first six shooters all failed to beat the two goalies, but Antoine Vermette scored on a backhander to start the fourth round and put the pressure on the Devils. Jamie Langenbrunner responded with a clutch goal, faking a deke and then firing a quick shot. Mike Comrie scored for Ottawa, but again, facing defeat, Sergei Brylin tied the shootout count. In the next round, Mike Fisher was stopped by Brodeur and Madden bettered Emery with a great top-shelf backhand to give the Devils two points.

Game 81

April 5, 2007
Pittsburgh 3 at Ottawa 2

By this point in the season, Ottawa and Pittsburgh knew their fate—they would be meeting each other in the first round of the playoffs. What they didn't know was which team would get home-ice advantage, and with this dramatic, last-minute win in Ottawa, the Penguins put themselves in a position to claim home ice for a potential game seven. Maxime Talbot was the hero this night, scoring the winning goal with just 9.8 seconds left on the Scotiabank Place scoreclock. Because of the impending playoff matchup, the game featured plenty of emotion and intensity. The opening period included eight minor penalties, one five-minute major, and two misconducts as both teams tried to work a psychological advantage heading to the post-season. Key among those violations was a set-to after Colby Armstrong ran into Ottawa goalie Ray Emery. A minuet later, more bad blood was spilled when Jason Spezza elbowed superpest Jarkko Ruutu. Spezza earned a major penalty on the play, and Pittsburgh cashed in with two power-play goals to wipe out a 1-0 lead which Spezza himself had given the Sens. His power-play goal at 7:59 opened the scoring, but Michel Ouellet and Gary Roberts scored a minute apart with him in the box serving his five minutes. There were eight more minor penalties in the second, but although the Sens peppered Marc-Andre Fleury with 19 shots in the middle 20 minutes, they managed only one goal, that an early power-play marker from Dany Heatley. It was his 49th goal of the year. The teams settled down in the third, but as overtime loomed Talbot beat Emery with a high shot while the teams were playing four-on-four. That left both Ottawa and Pittsburgh with 103 points in the standings and home-ice advantage still very much up in the air heading into the final game of the season.

Wade Redden (left) and Dany Heatley celebrate a goal against Boston on the final day of the regular season.

Game 82

April 7, 2007
Ottawa 6 at Boston 3

The Senators earned home-ice advantage for the first round of the playoffs by beating the Bruins in convincing fashion. Had they lost tonight, Pittsburgh would have opened the series at home against the Sens. In the process, Dany Heatley scored his 50th goal of the year to become the first player since Pavel Bure in 1999-2001 to record consecutive 50-goal seasons. His was the go-ahead goal after which the Sens never looked back. Ray Emery picked up his 33rd win of the year, and the big line of Heatley-Jason Spezza-Daniel Alfredsson was firing on all cylinders. In all, the three racked up eight points on this regular-season finale. Boston, meanwhile, was going golfing after this meaningless game to end a disappointing season. The game featured four goals before the seven-minute mark, two apiece. Marco Sturm made it 1-0 for Boston at 1:28, but Mike Comrie tied the game just two minutes later when Tim Thomas mishandled the puck behind his own net. Peter Kalus and Spezza exchanged similarly quick goals, and then the teams settled in to a comfortable pace. The next goal didn't come for 20 minutes. Heatley got the puck in the centre-ice area and skated down the right side. He saw Spezza going to the middle but fired away. The shot deflected off a Boston player in front and past Tim Thomas to give Ottawa a 3-2 lead and Heatley a place in the history books. The Bruins made it 4-3 with a power-play goal early in the third, but Ottawa scored the final two goals and pulled away for the win. Alfredsson scored at 6:18 on a two-man advantage, and Patrick Eaves closed out the scoring three minutes later. The Senators finished the regular season with a record of 48-25-9, good for fourth place and 105 points in the Eastern Conference standings.

The Players: 2006-07, Regular Season

Alfredsson, Daniel   b. Goteborg, Sweden, December 11, 1972
2006-07 OTT	77	29	58	87	42
NHL Totals	783	291	467	758	351

~drafted 133rd overall by Ottawa in 1994

Bois, Danny   b. Thunder Bay, Ontario, June 1, 1983
2006-07 OTT	1	0	0	0	7
NHL Totals	1	0	0	0	7

~recalled December 6, 2006 from Binghamton on emergency basis for Daniel Alfredsson

Comrie, Mike   b. Edmonton, Alberta, September 11, 1980
2006-07 PHO/OTT	65	20	25	45	44
NHL Totals	386	123	139	262	276

~acquired by Ottawa from Phoenix for Alexei Kaigorodov on January 3, 2007

Corvo, Joe   b. Oak Park, Illinois, June 20, 1977
2006-07 OTT	76	8	29	37	42
NHL Totals	279	35	79	114	130

~signed as a free agent by Ottawa on July 1, 2006

Eaves, Patrick   b. Calgary, Alberta, May 1, 1984
2006-07 OTT	73	14	18	32	36
NHL Totals	131	34	27	61	58

~drafted 29th overall by Ottawa in 2003

Emery, Ray   b. Cayuga, Ontario, September 28, 1982
2006-07 OTT	58	33-16-0-6	3,351	138	5	2.47
NHL Totals	103	59-27-0-10	5,729	247	8	2.59

~drafted 99th overall by Ottawa in 2001

Fisher, Mike   b. Peterborough, Ontario, June 5, 1980
2006-07 OTT	68	22	26	48	41
NHL Totals	384	92	100	192	314

~drafted 44th overall by Ottawa in 1998

Gerber, Martin   b. Burgdorf, Switzerland, September 3, 1974
2006-07 OTT	29	15-9-0-3	1,598	74	1	2.78
NHL Totals	143	70-46-7-9	7,993	339	7	2.54

~signed as a free agent by Ottawa on July 1, 2006

Hamel, Denis   b. Lachute, Quebec, May 10, 1977
2006-07 OTT/ATL/PHI	53	5	3	8	10
NHL Totals	192	19	12	31	77

~signed as a free agent by Ottawa on August 2, 2005; claimed on waivers by Atlanta from Ottawa on February 10, 2007; claimed on waivers by Philadelphia from Atlanta on February 27, 2007

Heatley, Dany   b. Freiburg, West Germany (Germany), January 21, 1981
2006-07 OTT	82	50	55	105	74
NHL Totals	354	180	209	389	292

~traded to Ottawa by Atlanta for Marian Hossa and Greg de Vries on August 23, 2005

Hennessy, Joshua   b. Brockton, Massachusetts, February 7, 1985
2006-07 OTT	10	1	0	1	4
NHL Totals	10	1	0	1	4

~recalled from Binghamton on December 12, 2006; sent to Binghamton on December 15; recalled from Binghamton on December 29; sent to Binghamton on January 4, 2007; recalled from Binghamton on January 6; sent to Binghamton on January 7; recalled from Binghamton on January 9; sent to Binghamton on January 12

Kaigorodov, Alexei   b. Chelyabinsk, Soviet Union (Russia), July 29, 1983
2006-07 OTT	6	0	1	1	0
NHL Totals	6	0	1	1	0

~traded by Ottawa to Phoenix for Mike Comrie on January 3, 2007

Kelly, Chris   b. Toronto, Ontario, November 11, 1980
2006-07 OTT	82	15	23	38	40
NHL Totals	168	25	43	68	116

~drafted 94th overall by Ottawa in 1999

Malec, Tomas   b. Skalica, Czechoslovakia (Slovakia), May 13, 1982
2006-07 OTT	1	0	0	0	0
NHL Totals	46	0	2	2	47

~signed as a free agent on August 19, 2005; traded by Ottawa to NY Islanders for Matt Koalska on January 5, 2007

McAmmond, Dean b Grand Cache, Alberta, June 15, 1973
2006-07 OTT	81	14	15	29	28
NHL Totals	804	164	229	393	414

~signed as a free agent on February 8, 2006

McGratton, Brian b. Hamilton, Ontario, September 2, 1981
2006-07 OTT	45	0	2	2	100
NHL Totals	105	2	5	7	241

~signed as a free agent on June 2, 2002

Meszaros, Andrei b. Povazska Bystrica, Czechoslovakia (Slovakia), October 13, 1985
2006-07 OTT	82	7	28	35	102
NHL Totals	164	17	57	74	163

~drafted 23rd overall by Ottawa in 2004

Neil, Chris b. Markdale, Ontario, June 18, 1979
2006-07 OTT	82	12	16	28	177
NHL Totals	383	52	52	104	953

~drafted 161st overall by Ottawa in 1998

Nycholat, Lawrence b. Calgary, Alberta, May 7, 1979
2006-07 WAS/OTT	19	2	6	8	12
NHL Totals	28	2	6	8	18

~traded to Ottawa by Washington for Andy Hedlund and a 6th-round draft choice in 2007 on February 26, 2007

Payer, Serge b. Rockland, Ontario, May 7, 1979
2006-07 OTT	5	0	0	0	0
NHL Totals	124	7	6	13	49

~signed as a free agent by Ottawa on August 2, 2006

Phillips, Chris b. Calgary, Alberta, March 9, 1978
2006-07 OTT	82	8	18	26	80
NHL Totals	618	40	124	164	456

~drafted 1st overall by Ottawa in 1996

Preissing, Tom b. Rosemount, Minnesota, December 3, 1978
2006-07 OTT	80	7	31	38	18
NHL Totals	223	20	80	100	56

~Ottawa traded Martin Havlat and Bryan Smolinski to Chicago; San Jose traded Tom Preissing and Josh Hennessy to Ottawa; Chicago traded Mark Bell to San Jose and Michal Barinka and a 2nd-round draft choice in 2008 to Ottawa, on July 9, 2006

Redden, Wade b Lloydminster, Saskatchewan, June 12, 1977
2006-07 OTT	64	7	29	36	50
NHL Totals	758	95	277	372	516

~traded to Ottawa from New York Islanders with Damian Rhodes for Bryan Berard, Don Beaupre, and Martin Straka on January 23, 1996

Saprykin, Oleg b. Moscow, Soviet Union (Russia), February 12, 1981
2006-07 PHO/OTT	71	15	21	36	58
NHL Totals	325	55	82	137	240

~traded to Ottawa by Phoenix with a 7th-round draft choice in 2007 for Ottawa's 2nd-round draft choice in 2008 on February 27, 2007

Schaefer, Peter b. Yellow Grass, Saskatchewan, July 12, 1977
2006-07 OTT	77	12	34	46	32
NHL Totals	493	89	144	233	180

~traded to Ottawa from Vancouver for Sami Salo on September 21, 2002

Schubert, Christoph b. Munich, (West) Germany, February 5, 1982
2006-07 OTT	80	8	17	25	56
NHL Totals	136	12	23	35	104

~drafted 127th overall by Ottawa in 2001

Spezza, Jason b. Mississauga, Ontario, June 13, 1983
2006-07 OTT	67	34	53	87	45
NHL Totals	246	82	171	253	157

~drafted 2nd overall by Ottawa in 2001

Vermette, Antoine b. St. Agapit, Quebec, July 20, 1982
2006-07 OTT	77	19	20	39	52
NHL Totals	216	47	39	86	112

~drafted 55th overall by Ottawa in 2000

Volchenkov, Anton b. Moscow, Soviet Union (Russia), February 25, 1982
2006-07 OTT	78	1	18	19	67
NHL Totals	229	9	46	55	168

~drafted 21st overall by Ottawa in 2000

Final Statistics, 2007 Playoffs

#	Pos	Name	GP	G	A	P	Pim
11	F	Daniel Alfredsson	20	14	8	22	10
15	F	Dany Heatley	20	7	15	22	14
19	F	Jason Spezza	20	7	15	22	10
12	F	Mike Fisher	20	5	5	10	24
6	D	Wade Redden	20	3	7	10	10
7	D	Joe Corvo	20	2	7	9	6
37	F	Dean McAmmond	18	5	3	8	11
22	F	Chris Kelly	20	3	4	7	4
42	D	Tom Preissing	20	2	5	7	10
14	D	Andrej Meszaros	20	1	6	7	12
24	D	Anton Volchenkov	20	2	4	6	24
89	F	Mike Comrie	20	2	4	6	17
27	F	Peter Schaefer	20	1	5	6	10
20	F	Antoine Vermette	20	2	3	5	6
25	F	Chris Neil	20	2	2	4	20
61	F	Oleg Saprykin	15	1	1	2	4
44	F	Patrick Eaves	7	0	2	2	2
1	G	Ray Emery	20	0	2	2	0
5	D	Christoph Schubert	20	0	1	1	22
4	D	Chris Phillips	20	0	0	0	24

In Goal

	GP	W-L	Mins	GA	SO	GAA
Ray Emery	20	13-7	1,248:37	47	3	2.26

Final Standings, 2006-07

Eastern Conference

	GP	W	L	OT	GF	GA	P
Atlantic Division							
New Jersey	82	49	24	9	216	201	107
Pittsburgh	82	47	24	11	277	246	105
NY Rangers	82	42	30	10	242	216	94
NY Islanders	82	40	30	12	248	240	92
Philadelphia	82	22	48	12	214	303	56
Northeast Division							
Buffalo	82	53	22	7	308	242	113
Ottawa	82	48	25	9	288	222	105
Toronto	82	40	31	11	258	269	91
Montreal	82	42	34	6	245	256	90
Boston	82	35	41	6	219	289	76
Southeast Division							
Atlanta	82	43	28	11	246	245	97
Tampa Bay	82	44	33	5	253	261	93
Carolina	82	40	34	8	241	253	88
Florida	82	35	31	16	247	257	86
Washington	82	28	40	14	235	286	70

Western Conference

	GP	W	L	OT	GF	GA	P
Central Division							
Detroit	82	50	19	13	254	199	113
Nashville	82	51	23	8	272	212	110
St. Louis	82	34	35	13	214	254	81
Columbus	82	33	42	7	201	249	73
Chicago	82	31	42	9	201	258	71
Northwest Division							
Vancouver	82	49	26	7	222	201	105
Minnesota	82	48	26	8	235	191	104
Calgary	82	43	29	10	258	226	96
Colorado	82	44	31	7	272	251	95
Edmonton	82	32	43	7	195	248	71
Pacific Division							
Anaheim	82	48	20	14	258	208	110
San Jose	82	51	26	5	258	199	107
Dallas	82	50	25	7	226	197	107
Los Angeles	82	27	41	14	227	283	68
Phoenix	82	31	46	5	216	284	67

2007 Playoff Results

Eastern Conference Quarter-finals

New York Islanders vs. **Buffalo Sabres**

April 12	NY Islanders 1 at Buffalo 4
April 14	NY Islanders 3 at Buffalo 2
April 16	Buffalo 3 at NY Islanders 2
April 18	Buffalo 4 at NY Islanders 2
April 20	NY Islanders 3 at Buffalo 4

Buffalo wins best-of-seven 4-1

Tampa Bay Lightning vs. **New Jersey Devils**

April 12	Tampa Bay 3 at New Jersey 5
April 14	Tampa Bay 3 at New Jersey 2
April 16	New Jersey 2 at Tampa Bay 3
April 18	New Jersey 4 at Tampa Bay 3 (Gomez 12:54 OT)
April 20	Tampa Bay 0 at New Jersey 3 [Brodeur]
April 22	New Jersey 3 at Tampa Bay 2

New Jersey wins best-of-seven 4-2

New York Rangers vs. **Atlanta Thrashers**

April 12	NY Rangers 4 at Atlanta 3
April 14	NY Rangers 2 at Atlanta 1
April 17	Atlanta 0 at NY Rangers 7 [Lundqvist]
April 18	Atlanta 2 at NY Rangers 4

NY Rangers win best-of-seven 4-0

Pittsburgh Penguins vs. **Ottawa Senators**

April 11	Pittsburgh 3 at Ottawa 6
April 14	Pittsburgh 4 at Ottawa 3
April 15	Ottawa 4 at Pittsburgh 2
April 17	Ottawa 2 at Pittsburgh 1
April 19	Pittsburgh 0 at Ottawa 3 [Emery]

Ottawa wins best-of-seven 4-1

Western Conference Quarter-finals

Calgary Flames vs. **Detroit Red Wings**

April 12	Calgary 1 at Detroit 4
April 15	Calgary 1 at Detroit 3
April 17	Detroit 2 at Calgary 3
April 19	Detroit 2 at Calgary 3
April 21	Calgary 1 at Detroit 5
April 22	Detroit 2 at Calgary 1 (Franzen 24:23 OT)

Detroit wins best-of-seven 4-2

Minnesota Wild vs. **Anaheim Ducks**

April 11	Minnesota 1 at Anaheim 2
April 13	Minnesota 2 at Anaheim 3
April 15	Anaheim 2 at Minnesota 1
April 17	Anaheim 1 at Minnesota 4
April 19	Minnesota 1 at Anaheim 4

Anaheim wins best-of-seven 4-1

Dallas Stars vs. **Vancouver Canucks**

April 11	Dallas 4 at Vancouver 5 (H. Sedin 78:06 OT)
April 13	Dallas 2 at Vancouver 0 [Turco]
April 15	Vancouver 2 at Dallas 1 (Pyatt 7:47 OT)
April 17	Vancouver 2 at Dallas 1
April 19	Dallas 1 at Vancouver 0 (Morrow 6:22 OT)/[Turco]
April 21	Vancouver 0 at Dallas 2 [Turco]
April 23	Dallas 1 at Vancouver 4

Vancouver wins best-of-seven 4-3

San Jose Sharks vs. **Nashville Predators**

April 11	San Jose 5 at Nashville 4 (Rissmiller 28:14 OT)
April 13	San Jose 2 at Nashville 5
April 16	Nashville 1 at San Jose 3
April 18	Nashville 2 at San Jose 3
April 20	San Jose 3 at Nashville 2

San Jose wins best-of-seven 4-1

Eastern Conference Semi-finals

Ottawa Senators vs. **New Jersey Devils**

April 26	Ottawa 5 at New Jersey 4
April 28	Ottawa 2 at New Jersey 3 (Langenbrunner 21:55 OT)
April 30	New Jersey 0 at Ottawa 2 [Emery]
May 2	New Jersey 2 at Ottawa 3
May 5	Ottawa 3 at New Jersey 2

Ottawa wins best-of-seven 4-1

New York Rangers vs. **Buffalo Sabres**

April 25	NY Rangers 2 at Buffalo 5
April 27	NY Rangers 2 at Buffalo 3
April 29	Buffalo 1 at NY Rangers 2 (Rozsival 36:43 OT)
May 1	Buffalo 1 at NY Rangers 2
May 4	NY Rangers 1 at Buffalo 2 (Afinogenov 4:39 OT)
May 6	Buffalo 5 at NY Rangers 4

Buffalo wins best-of-seven 4-2

Western Conference Semi-finals

Vancouver Canucks vs **Anaheim Ducks**

April 25	Vancouver 1 at Anaheim 5
April 27	Vancouver 2 at Anaheim 1 (Cowan 27:49 OT)
April 29	Anaheim 3 at Vancouver 2
May 1	Anaheim 3 at Vancouver 2 (Moen 2:07 OT)
May 3	Vancouver 1 at Anaheim 2 (S. Niedermayer 24:30 OT)

Anaheim wins best-of-seven 4-1

San Jose Sharks vs **Detroit Red Wings**

April 26	San Jose 2 at Detroit 0 [Nabokov]
April 28	San Jose 2 at Detroit 3
April 30	Detroit 1 at San Jose 2
May 2	Detroit 3 at San Jose 2 (Schneider 16:04 OT)
May 5	San Jose 1 at Detroit 4
May 7	Detroit 2 at San Jose 0 [Hasek]

Detroit wins best-of-seven 4-2

Eastern Conference Finals

Ottawa Senators vs. **Buffalo Sabres**

May 10	Ottawa 5 at Buffalo 2
May 12	Ottawa 4 at Buffalo 3 (Corvo 24:58 OT)
May 14	Buffalo 0 at Ottawa 1 (Alfredsson 13:40 2nd) [Emery]
May 10	Ottawa 5 at Buffalo 2
May 12	Ottawa 4 at Buffalo 3 (Corvo 24:58 OT)
May 14	Buffalo 0 at Ottawa 1 (Alfredsson 13:40 2nd) [Emery]
May 16	Buffalo 3 at Ottawa 2
May 19	Ottawa 3 at Buffalo 2

Ottawa wins best-of-seven 4-1

Western Conference Finals

Anaheim Ducks vs. **Detroit Red Wings**

May 11	Anaheim 1 at Detroit 2
May 13	Anaheim 4 at Detroit 3 (S. Niedermayer 14:17 OT)
May 15	Detroit 5 at Anaheim 0 [Hasek]
May 17	Detroit 3 at Anaheim 5
May 20	Anaheim 2 at Detroit 1 (Selanne 11:57 OT)
May 22	Detroit 3 at Anaheim 4

Anaheim wins best-of-seven 4-2

Stanley Cup Finals

Ottawa Senators vs. **Anaheim Ducks**

May 28	Ottawa 2 at Anaheim 3
May 30	Ottawa 0 at Anaheim 1 [Giguere]
June 2	Anaheim 3 at Ottawa 5
June 4	Anaheim 3 at Ottawa 2
June 6	Ottawa 2 at Anaheim 6

Anaheim wins best-of-seven 4-1

Conference Quarter-finals
Pittsburgh Penguins vs. Ottawa Senators

Game 1

April 11, 2007
Pittsburgh 3 at Ottawa 6

Let's face it. Prior to the first game of the playoffs, no one quite knew what to expect in this series. For Ottawa fans, the team had an excellent year but had shown weaknesses, and its playoff history was consistently disappointing. Yet, this was a team that looked like it could be great. Pittsburgh was in the playoffs for the first time in six years, and it had a lineup featuring 13 players who were about to play their first post-season game. One of those players, though, was Sidney Crosby, and during his first two years in the NHL he had proved, if nothing else, that when people thought he was in over his head he, in fact, excelled. This regular season he led all players with 120 points, the youngest ever to win the Art Ross Trophy, and as he went so went the Penguins. It was that simple. And so it was that in his first game of his playoff career, he ended up on the losing end, but for a bit of luck the result might have been different. Crosby scored a goal late in the game that had little meaning, but he also had another called back at a time when it might have had great meaning. More than that, though, the Senators executed. Their scorers scored; their defence played well inside its blueline; and, for the most part, goalie Ray Emery stopped what

Chris Neil beats Marc-Andre Fleury during Ottawa's relatively easy win in game one against the Penguins.

was thrown his way. In the end, the score flattered the Penguins who trailed 3-0 halfway through the game and 6-1 with eight minutes left. For Ottawa, the game was a success on many levels. They got goals from six different players; their power play worked well; they played with confidence whey then had a lead, something they had had trouble with during the regular season at times. The Sens got off to a flying start, scoring the only two goals of the first period. The opening shot was fired by Andrej Meszaros just 97 seconds into the game when he had an open net and goalie Marc-Andre Fleury on the ice during a scramble. Meszaros made no mistake, and the early score sent the 19,611 fans at Scotiabank Place into a frenzy. The Sens made it 2-0 on a nice play from Chris Kelly. Joe Corvo took a shot that was blocked by Pittsburgh defenceman Mark Eaton, but Kelly got the puck with Eaton on his knees and his quick shot beat Fleury cleanly. Tom Preissing scored on a power play late in the second, but Jordan Staal made the game a little closer with a goal at 16:58 to make it 3-1. The early part of the third period sealed the Penguins' fate. First, they allowed a Dany Heatley power-play goal just nine seconds into the period with Crosby in the box, and then Crosby scored a goal a couple of minutes later which would have made it a 4-2 game. Video review, however, indicated he kicked the puck in, and Ottawa went on to score two more goals. Chris Neil and Mike Comrie put the game out of reach, and only then did Pittsburgh score again. Sergei Gonchar connected on the power play to make it 6-2, and then Crosby got one that counted, in the final minute. All in all, it was an excellent start for Ottawa as the team played its game to perfection and refused to allow Crosby to have any influence on the game's outcome.

Ottawa leads best-of-seven 1-0

Chris Phillips plays physically against Sidney Crosby.

Conference Quarter-finals: Pittsburgh Penguins vs. Ottawa Senators

Game 2
April 14, 2007
Pittsburgh 4 at Ottawa 3

The old bad habit of playing poorly with a lead came back to haunt the Ottawa bench during game two of this series, and the Senators paid a dear price for it. They failed to hold a lead after two periods, and when they got another lead early in the third, they managed to lose the game all the same. Sidney Crosby, quiet in game one, had a huge goal and assist tonight, but he was helped by excellent performances from most of his teammates. For Ottawa, this was a game they lost more than the Penguins won. In seven previous playoff series in which they won the first game, the Senators failed to win game two each and every time. Theirs was a psychological battle right now as much as physical, although within the game the power play was certainly a factor. Ottawa scored only once on nine chances; Pittsburgh struck twice on just three opportunities. The Penguins' Ryan Whitney got the first goal just 3:01 into the game with Daniel Alfredsson in the box for goalie interference. The lead help up until midway through the second when Jason Spezza evened the count for Ottawa while the teams were playing four skaters a

Crosby gets the shaft of his stick on Mark Recchi's cross-ice pass for the winning goal in the third period of game two.

Conference Quarter-finals: **Pittsburgh Penguins** vs. **Ottawa Senators**

Patrick Eaves makes a sensational defensive play, clearing the puck off the line to prevent a goal.

side. The Senators took the lead later in the period on a great set-up by Dany Heatley for Alfredsson on the power play. The Ottawa captain teed up a perfect feed from Heatley and hit the open side of the net before goalie Marc-Andre Fleury could come across the crease. Despite heading to the dressing room after two periods with a one-goal lead, though, the Senators allowed Pittsburgh back in the game early in the final period. Gary Roberts banged home a rebound when he was left unguarded just 2:04 into the period to tie the game at 2-2. Chris Kelly gave the Senators another lead at 6:18, but again Ottawa couldn't close out the game. Tenacious forechecking by Roberts behind the Ottawa goal forced defenceman Wade Redden to cough up the puck, and Michel Ouellet came in to give Roberts a hand. His quick pass to Jordan Staal out front was perfect, and Staal made no mistake with his chance, beating Ray Emery with a quick, hard shot to make it 3-3. That set the stage for Crosby. Mark Recchi carried the puck over the Ottawa blueline and watched as Sid the Kid skated full speed to the crease. Recchi made a perfect pass to Crosby, and he redirected the puck past Emery to score what proved to be the game-winning goal. Less than a minute later, Ottawa had a power play thanks to an Evgeni Malkin penalty for holding the stick, but the Sens came up short. Despite outshooting Pittsburgh 31-16 over the last two periods, Ottawa couldn't beat Fleury, who atoned for a mediocre outing in game one.

Best-of-seven tied 1-1

A mad scramble in front of goalie Ray Emery sees Sidney Crosby and Mark Recchi battle defenceman Anton Volchenkov.

Game 3

April 15, 2007
Ottawa 4 at Pittsburgh 2

Playing back-to-back games used to be the norm in the NHL, but not so in the 21st century. Yet here were Pittsburgh and Ottawa traveling after game two get ready for another game less than 24 hours later. Ah, the good old days! The Senators may have taken a few minutes to get their legs, but they scored four goals in succession during the middle part of the game to win this handily. Trying to get the crowd into the game, Gary Roberts picked up where he left off in Ottawa, scoring the first goal in the first minute of the game to give the Penguins an early need. The setback had little negative impact on Ottawa, though, and the Sens simply got their legs and started to play their game with greater and greater confidence. Dean McAmmond tied the game later in the period when he went to the net on a Patrick Eaves shot. Goalie Marc-Andre Fleury made the save, but when he failed to control the rebound McAmmond was right there to capitalize. Despite the evenly-played opening 20 minutes, the Penguins came out flat in the second and were unable to cope with Ottawa's speed and determination. The Senators scored three times in the middle period to pull away, perhaps catching the Pens off guard and certainly putting them in a hole. Mike Comrie got things started with a timely goal at 2:13. Joe Corvo took a point shot that Fleury was ready for, but it bounced off a couple of players in front and landed on Comrie's stick. Fleury was out of position, and the Ottawa forward had no trouble putting the puck in the open side of the net. Five minutes later, Daniel Alfredsson scored on the power play with a great shot, and later in the period he struck again when he connected with a beautiful one-timer off a pass from Dean McAmmond just as Comrie was coming out of the penalty box. Sidney Crosby got one goal back in the third, but it was too little, too late. The goal nonetheless was a typical Crosby treat, scored while he was on his behind but managing to get a great shot away all the same. The Penguins couldn't continue to charge after this goal, and with the win Ottawa reclaimed home-ice advantage. More important, the team played with a confidence that Pittsburgh couldn't match. The Senators contained Crosby well, and they all but eliminated rookie sensation Evgeni Malkin, who had not been a factor at all in the first three games.

Ottawa leads best-of-seven 2-1

Dany Heatley and Daniel Alfredsson celebrate an Ottawa goal as a disconsolate Marc-Andre Fleury reacts in the background.

Conference Quarter-finals: Pittsburgh Penguins vs. Ottawa Senators

Game 4

April 17, 2007
Ottawa 2 at Pittsburgh 1

There were three mini-games played in game four: the first saw an evenly-played opening period; the second was a 20-minute session dominated by Pittsburgh; and, the third was a great performance by Ottawa which gave the Senators a 2-1 win and a 3-1 series stranglehold heading home for the fifth game. Sidney Crosby was held without a goal for the first time, and Evgeni Malkin was still looking for his first of the post-season. Ray Emery stopped 23 of 24 shots and was sensational in goal for the Senators. Ottawa got the only goal of a wide open and entertaining first period. Jason Spezza had the puck off to the side of the net on a power play, and his hard pass through the slot hit Jordan Staal's stick and past a

Gary Roberts and Jordan Staal try to beat Ray Emery in close. Staal succeeds, scoring Pittsburgh's only goal of the game.

Conference Quarter-finals: **Pittsburgh Penguins vs. Ottawa Senators**

Ryan Malone tries a wraparound but Ray Emery is there to block the shot.

helpless Marc-Andre Fleury. It was a lucky goal, to be sure, but the breaks are part of the game and Ottawa was happy to accept this one. Pittsburgh came out flying in the second and dominated for most of the 20 minutes. The Penguins tied the game midway through when Staal scored one for his own team. Michel Ouellet had the puck behind the Ottawa net and made a nice play to get the puck in front. He had the option of either Gary Roberts or Staal, but Staal made the choice for him and got first stick on the puck. He made a perfect shot to beat Emery cleanly at 8:08. Pittsburgh continued to attack the rest of the period, outshooting Ottawa, 13-4. The Senators also took the only four penalties of the period, but the usually potent Pittsburgh power play could not gain the lead and Ottawa was fortunate to be in a 1-1 tie after 40 minutes. The Senators came out to start the third knowing the series was on the line for the Penguins. Pittsburgh could not have realistic hopes of winning the series if it trailed 3-1 and had to play game five in Ottawa. The Senators got the goal they needed midway through the period. Mike Comrie skated around the Pittsburgh goal and as he slid toward the corner boards he fired a hard pass to defenceman Anton Volchenkov who broke in from the blueline. The pass was perfect, and Volchenkov snapped off a one-timer that went over Fleury's shoulder to give Ottawa the lead. Volchenkov had only one goal all year (in 78 games), but his timing for goal number two could not have been finer. Ottawa played masterful hockey the rest of the way and went home knowing the series was theirs for the taking.

Ottawa leads best-of-seven 3-1

Game 5
April 19, 2007
Pittsburgh 0 at **Ottawa** 3

A blistering second period which produced three goals from different scorers. A great performance by goalie Ray Emery. And, a team defence that shut down Sidney Crosby and Evgeni Malkin. All these were elements that gave Ottawa a win in the game and the series. The start of the game, though, was the difference. Ottawa incurred three minor penalties in the first three and a half minutes, but the refereeing had little to do with the calls. Wade Redden received a tripping call at 1:00, but then two Senators—Dean McAmmond and Christoph Schubert—cleared the puck over the glass. These are automatic calls, and Pittsburgh had two five-on-three situations. Nevertheless, the Ottawa penalty killers stood tall and weathered the storm, and goalie Ray Emery was sharp. Even though shots were 7-0 for the Penguins through the first half of the period, the score remained 0-0. Buoyed by their survival of this rough start, the Senators picked up the pace, stayed out of the penalty box, and started taking the play to Pittsburgh. They dominated the last half of the first, and in the second they took control, scoring the only three goals they would need to eliminate Pittsburgh. Dany Heatley started the offense early in the period on the power play. Parked to the side of the net, he took a Daniel Alfredsson pass and buried it before Marc-Andre Fleury could move over. The goal deflated the Penguins, and Ottawa kept coming. Antoine Vermette made it 2-0 when he charged to the net and beat Fleury with a shot, and Chris Kelly put the icing on the cake at 17:55. In the third, Pittsburgh again had two early extra-man opportunities, but again they failed to score. Emery earned his first career playoff shutout, and kudos went out to the defensive tandem of Chris Phillips and Anton Volchenkov who had done such a good job shadowing Crosby for five games. Evgeni Malkin went home still looking for his first playoff goal. It might well be that the young and inexperienced Penguins had some learning to do before they could win in the post-season, but for the ten

Antoine Vermette scores a gorgeous goal, beating Marc-Andre Fleury while falling to the ice.

Penguins star Evegni Malkin is cleared from Ray Emery's crease by Daniel Alfredsson (left) and Anton Volchenkov.

days of this series Ottawa was simply the superior team in all aspects. Most important for the Senators, they played with poise and maturity. There were several key moments when they might have collapsed or lost their cool, but they never did. They also got goals from eleven different players, a key element to any success in the playoffs. And, by making short work of the Penguins, they assured themselves of a week's worth of rest and recuperation before the start of their next series.

Ottawa wins best-of-seven 4-1

Conference Quarter-finals: **Pittsburgh Penguins** vs. **Ottawa Senators**

Conference Semi-finals
Ottawa Senators vs. New Jersey Devils

Game 1

April 26, 2007
Ottawa 5 at New Jersey 4

As they had done early in the year, Ottawa got to New Jersey goalie Martin Brodeur in game one of this series. Unlike that game, however, which turned into an 8-1 romp, the Senators nearly blew a huge 4-0 lead this night. The Sens managed to hold on, but by game's end they hadn't quite the same confidence that had as, say, late in the first period. Any team that wants to have a chance to assert its own game must get the first goal against the Devils. If the Devils score first, they will play a game of stifling defence that makes it more and more difficult to score as the game goes on. Kudos to the Senators, then, for going to the attack on the road in game one of a series and not starting tentatively. They were rewarded early when a Tom Preissing shot was deflected ever so slightly by Jason Spezza, enough to

Jason Spezza and Richard Matvichuk look on as Martin Brodeur allows another goal during the Senators' 5-4 win to open the Conference semi-finals.

fool Brodeur and spot the Sens a 1-0 lead just 1:30 into the game. They made it 2-0 when Joe Corvo scored on the power play at 6:49, his hard shot catching Brodeur's glove but carrying into the net all the same. The Devils had possession but failed to clear the puck out of their end and paid for it with a goal. Most nights, Brodeur would have held onto the puck; this night, the bounce went Ottawa's way. The Senators upped the advantage to three goals at 14:43 when Dean McAmmond scored short-handed. He stripped Brian Rafalski of the puck and waltzed in alone on Brodeur, beating the goalie cleanly. Two minutes later, Dany Heatley carried the puck into the New Jersey end on a two-on-one after New Jersey lost possession near the Ottawa blueline, but rather than risk a pass he fired away and beat Brodeur again. The only ray of light for the Devils was a goal by Travis Zajac a minute later to make it 4-1. Jamie Langenbrunner made a nice pass to give Zajac the opportunity, but the Devils had put themselves in a serious hole. Brian Gionta and Andy Greene scored early in the second for the Devils, and with the score now 4-3 the team had a little life. Unlike games earlier in the season, though, or game two against Pittsburgh, Ottawa remained calm and stuck to its game plan. New Jersey never did get the tying goal. Instead, Wade Redden made it 5-3 early in the third on a power play to give the Sens a bit of breathing room, and only a last-minute goal by Zach Parise altered the scoreboard thereafter. Ottawa had done its job by taking home-ice advantage in the first game of the series, but there were two significant factors it had to concern itself with for game two. One, it couldn't rely on Brodeur having another weak game. In fact, just the opposite. The Sens had to expect Brodeur would be looking to avenge his poor outing with a sensational one, as he had during the regular season after the 8-1 loss. And two, the Sens could not possibly hope to win the series if it kept blowing leads or letting the other team back in the game. Ottawa needed a killer instinct. No mercy.

Ottawa leads best-of-seven 1-0

Dany Heatley raises his arms in joy as the Sens put another shot past Martin Brodeur.

Conference Semi-finals: Ottawa Senators vs. New Jersey Devils

Wade Redden (left) and Dany Heatley celebrate Heatley's goal in the final minute of regulation to send the game into overtime.

Game 2
April 28, 2007
Ottawa 2 at New Jersey 3 (2OT)

The adage that you can't win every game is all the more difficult to stomach in the playoffs when every game is so important, and every goal has the possibility of changing the complexion of the outcome of a game and series. For Ottawa to lose this game in double overtime was an unjust result, but the scoreboard is all that matters and on this night Ottawa fell a goal short of its just reward. New Jersey built a 2-0 lead after the first period, sat on the lead for the rest of the night only to find Ottawa dominating every aspect of the game, yet pulled out victory with a breakaway goal by Jamie Langenbrunner early in the second overtime period to tie the series, 1-1. The Devils made sure there was no

Conference Semi-finals: Ottawa Senators vs. New Jersey Devils

Jamie Langenbrunner scores the game-winning goal in the fifth period to tie the best-of-seven series 1-1.

first-period outburst by the Sens to start game two, and Ottawa gave a helping hand by incurring six minor penalties in the first, three of which resulted in power plays for New Jersey and two of which were assessed concurrently, giving New Jersey a five-on-three for the full two minutes. Brian Gionta scored on a power play just 1:43 into the game. He finished off a nice series of quick passes in the Ottawa end and notched his NHL-leading seventh goal of the playoffs. The Devils made it a 2-0 game on another power play, scoring with just 0.2 seconds left on the scoreclock courtesy of a bad defensive error by Jason Spezza. Sergei Brylin and Spezza lined up a faceoff in the Ottawa end with just 2.7 seconds on the clock. As the linesman dropped the puck, Brylin fell forward but got his stick on the puck. His quick shot fooled Emery, but had Spezza merely tied up his man, Brylin would never have scored. Video review confirmed the puck crossed the goal line before the end of the period. The Senators were furious, though, because they felt the timekeeper was slow to start the clock after the puck drop. Down but not out, the Senators came out to start the second with tremendous confidence. They scored the only goal of the period, and this time it was New Jersey that had a bit of penalty trouble as the Devils incurred the only three minors of the period. Daniel Alfredsson made it a 2-1 game at 4:23 when he took a pass from Spezza behind the net to the side boards. His quick shot caught Brodeur off guard. But try as the Senators might to tie the score, Brodeur would not allow another goal this period. The third was again all Ottawa, but Brodeur was sensational. Just as it looked as though the game would end 2-1, though, Ottawa pulled out all the stops. With Emery on the bench in the final minute, Spezza had the puck behind the goal. Although Dany Heatley was well covered in front, Spezza made the pass and Heatley got his stick on the puck enough to beat Brodeur and tie the game. In the first overtime, the Sens did everything but score the game winner, and in the second overtime, New Jersey did what Ottawa couldn't do. Travis Zajac made a pass half the length of the ice, from deep in his end to Langenbrunner coming up through centre ice. He shrugged off a check from Joe Corvo and moved in alone on Emery, and made no mistake with his shot. From the start of the second period to the end of the game, the Sens outshot New Jersey 40-17, yet Ottawa went home losers. That's the difference Martin Brodeur can make in a game.

Best-of-seven tied 1-1

Conference Semi-finals: Ottawa Senators vs. New Jersey Devils

Game 3

April 30, 2007
New Jersey 0 at **Ottawa** 2

The Ottawa Senators were playing with such confidence that they actually out-New Jerseyed the Devils in this game, playing sound defence and capitalizing on their one and only goal until they hit the empty net in the dying moments of the game. The win gave the Sens the series lead, and it was all the more rewarding because Martin Brodeur played a sensational game for the Devils. The goaltenders' battle was won by Ray Emery, something few could have predicted back at training camp in September 2006. Ottawa was clearly the better team all night and had the better opportunities. The Senators actually scored twice in the opening period, though neither goal counted. On the first play, Jason Spezza followed up his shot by going to the net and jamming the loose puck across the goal line, but referee Kelly Sutherland ruled the whistle had stopped play before the puck entered the net. The second chance was a goal, but it went into the net after the expiration of the first period. Nonetheless, the Senators held the edge in play and came at the Devils aggressively when the opportunity presented itself. When it didn't, they didn't try to force matters. The Devils sat back confident of playing a goalless game, confident Ottawa would make the one needed error for the Devils to take advantage of. There were precious few penalties called, and the lack of power play time, while refreshing, also helped keep the game scoreless. Both teams had some scoring chances in the second period, but it was a controversial play early in the third that led to the first legitimate goal of the night. Tom Preissing took a harmless-looking shot from near the end red line to Brodeur's glove side, and somehow the goalie flubbed the puck and it went in. Brodeur complained to the officials that he had been interfered with, and, indeed, Mike Fisher acknowledged that he had made accidental contact with Brodeur, upsetting the goalie's positioning just enough to be a distraction. The goal stood, however, and the Senators had the lead they needed at 4:46 of the third. They had to kill off two penalties later in the period—one to Oleg Saprykin, the other to Chris Phillips—and then in the final minute, with Brodeur on the bench for a sixth attacker, Jason Spezza scored into the open net to send the 19,636 Scotiabank Place fans into a frenzy. Ray Emery stopped 25 shots for the shutout, and the Senators played what might have been their most perfect game of the season.

Peter Schaefer takes some high fives after a Senators goal.

Mike Comrie takes a spill as Martin Brodeur blocks his path and controls the puck.

Game 4

May 2, 2007
New Jersey 2 at **Ottawa 3**

Of course, any time a talented team plays well, it feels it should win. The reality is often quite different, though, but not now, not for Ottawa. The Senators were not only playing well—they were getting the breaks. In the end, they took a commanding 3-1 series lead over New Jersey and put themselves in a position to eliminate the Devils three days later and earn more valuable rest as well. Tonight, it was a Dany Heatley goal that was huge, a shot that Martin Brodeur would have stopped the next thousand times he faced it. Daniel Alfredsson scored the game's first goal—and the only goal of the

Chris Neil crashes into Brodeur as Brad Lukowich skates by.

Conference Semi-finals: Ottawa Senators vs. New Jersey Devils

Jason Spezza reacts as the Senators put a goal past Martin Brodeur in their 3-2 win.

opening period—when he combined with linemates Heatley and Jason Spezza at 4:34. Alfredsson took a pass from Spezza, moved the puck along the boards in the New Jersey end, and went to the net as Heatley controlled the puck behind Brodeur. Heatley made the pass in front when Alfredsson was free, and the captain roofed a high shot that caught Brodeur by surprise. The Senators killed off all three minors in the first, the only penalties of the period. Brian Gionta got the Devils back on even terms with a goal early in the second. He got to the rebound of a Patrik Elias shot before Ray Emery could get set, and he made no mistake with the chance to tie the game, 1-1. Heatley's go-ahead goal later in the second was a tough pill for Brodeur and the Devils to swallow. Heatley was at a terrible angle to Brodeur's left and tried to make a pass through the crease to Spezza, but the puck banked off Brodeur's skate and between his pads at 14:44 to give the Sens a precious 2-1 lead. Mike Fisher increased the lead early in the third on another goal Brodeur would not normally allow. Fisher simply barreled down the wing and let fire a wrist shot from long range that handcuffed the goalie. The 3-1 score sent the record 20,248 fans at Scotiabank Place into riotous celebration, and the Devils had little hope of overcoming the Senators on this night. Jay Pandolfo got one goal back on a deflection which was allowed after video review, but then the Devils took two successive penalties to dull the momentum and kill any hopes of a tying goal. With Brodeur on the bench for an extra attacker, the Devils charged the Ottawa goal, but Emery remained poised and his defence surrounded him with all their might to preserve the win and take a 3-1 advantage to the Meadowlands for game five.

Ottawa leads best-of-seven 3-1

Fighting the puck all series, Martin Brodeur allows a soft goal from Daniel Alfredsson late in the second period that proved to be the game-winning score.

Game 5

May 5, 2007
Ottawa 3 at New Jersey 2

Another one-goal game, another goaltenders' battle won by the underdog, another opponent by the wayside as Ottawa advanced to the Conference finals for only the second time in its history. Although the Sens had made the playoffs for ten successive years, this was the first time the team seemed destined for something more than heartbreak and disappointment. This victory came about in many the same ways as others. The Senators remained calm after falling behind and they used an explosive second period to take control of the game. In some respects, the tuning point in the game came after the first period. The Sens were outshot in the opening 20 minutes by an 11-3 margin, trailed 1-0, and were lucky the Devils hadn't scored more. Only some key saves by Ray Emery and some poor finishing by the Devils prevented a barrage of goals. Still, the Senators knew they had dodged a bullet and came out to start the second like it was a new game. Indeed, they looked like a new team, and won the series in this middle 20 minutes. They scored three times, prevented the Devils from doing what they had done in the first—namely, go to the net with the puck—and headed to the dressing room knowing the series was within grasp. Scott Gomez opened the scoring when he got to a rebound of a Patrik Elias shot and jammed it home, but the rest of the game belonged to Ottawa. The Sens tied the game at 5:19 of the second thanks to two fine plays by Antoine Vermette. First, he controlled a puck near the Devils blueline that seemed

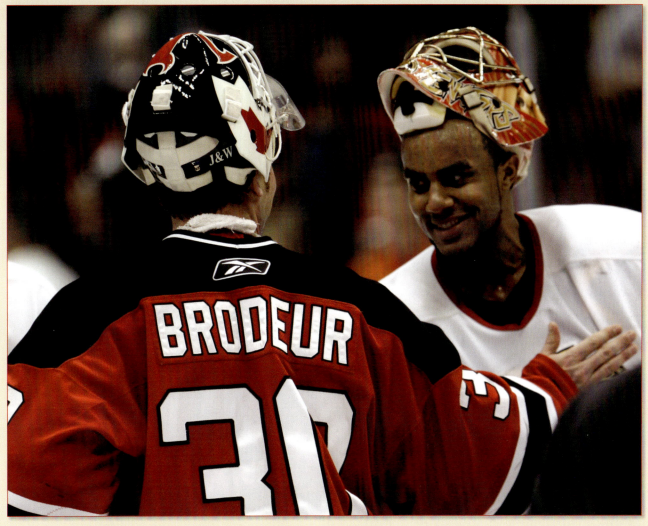
The goalies shake. Martin Brodeur and Ray Emery greet each other after the Senators eliminated the Devils.

destined to clear the area, and then he went to the net and made a great deflection of a Tom Preissing shot that Martin Brodeur couldn't stop. Jason Spezza gave the Sens their first lead on a power play with Jay Pandolfo in the box for goalie interference after he got tangled up with Emery. Spezza brought the puck off the boards, skated into the circle, and ripped a wrist shot through a maze of players that Brodeur couldn't see let alone stop. Daniel Alfredsson doubled the lead late in the period on another weak goal. He took a pass from Spezza just outside the blueline, moved in on goal and fired a quick shot from well out that found a space between Brodeur's pads. The goal took the crowd out of the game and had Brodeur wondering what was going on. Ottawa made no pretence about wanting to score in the third. The Sens had their lead; all they wanted was to get out of town with the series win. New Jersey outshot the Sens 9-2 in the third, but it was only a late goal by Gomez with 40 seconds to play that got past Emery. Brodeur was on the bench for that score and remained there for the final seconds, but the Devils could not pull off a miracle and were sent packing. Every game in this series was decided by one goal, except game three which was 2-0. Even that, though, was like a one-goal game because the second Ottawa goal went into the empty net. Ottawa, which had lost 22 of 32 one-goal games during the regular season, was now learning how to win the close games. And at just the right time, too.

Ottawa wins best-of-seven 4-1

Conference Finals
Ottawa Senators vs. Buffalo Sabres

Game 1
May 10, 2007
Ottawa 5 at Buffalo 2

Although the Buffalo Sabres led the regular season with 53 wins, they were facing a radically different Ottawa team than the one they eliminated comfortably in five games from the 2006 playoffs. The main difference was psychological more than anything, and this opening-game victory drove that point home. The Senators built a 2-0 only to give the goals back to Buffalo, but they remained poised and scored three unanswered markers in the third to pull away for an impressive win. Both teams had reason to be optimistic coming into this series. For Buffalo, the team was on a roll that started in training camp and never let up. For Ottawa, this was a team that won five of the eight regular-season meetings against the Sabres. The Senators knew that if they played smart hockey they could beat Buffalo, and that's what they did in game one. They got better goaltending, and they capitalized on their chances. Most important,

Daniel Alfredsson fights his way through to Buffalo goalie Ryan Miller.

Jason Spezza does a double-pelican to avoid a shot as Ryan Miller makes the save.

they didn't beat themselves. Point in case was the first goal of the game, scored by Mike Fisher. He stole the puck from a Buffalo defenceman just inside the Ottawa blueline on a Sabres' power play and raced in alone on a breakaway. Fisher calmly beat Ryan Miller for the opening score at 4:32 to silence the Buffalo crowd at HSBC Arena. Three minutes later, Ottawa did what Buffalo failed to do—score on the power play. This time it was captain Daniel Alfredsson. Buffalo got one goal back when Maxim Afinogenov beat Ray Emery with a shot, and in the second period the Sabres tied the score.

Toni Lydman got that goal at 8:45, and Buffalo was back in the game. Ottawa never panicked, though. The players headed to the dressing room after two periods in a 2-2 tie on enemy ice, and they felt good about their situation. The third period was almost entirely Ottawa's. The Sens scored the only three goals to pull away, and showed both a resilience and firepower that left the Sabres stunned. Oleg Saprykin got the go-ahead goal shortly after Emery made a big save off Adam Mair to keep it a 2-2 game. Saprykin made a great tip of a Dean McAmmond shot at 7:41, just the play the Senators needed. Jason Spezza scored on the power play later in the period, and McAmmond added a goal into the empty net. The win had several ramifications. The Sabres were badly outplayed and outshot (34-20) and went goalless on five power-play chances. Ottawa was 2-for-6 with the extra man. More amazingly, in Buffalo's playoff history, the team had lost 13 of 14 series after losing the first game, a sign that did not bode well for the usually resilient team of Lindy Ruff's.

Ottawa leads best-of-seven 1-0

Game 2

May 12, 2007
Ottawa 4 at Buffalo 3 (2 OT)

What an incredible roller-coaster of a night this was, but in the end the Senators did something they had never before done—they won game two of a series after winning the first game. In other words, for the first time ever, the Senators were leading a series 2-0, giving them an excellent chance to move on to the Stanley Cup finals. Buffalo would now have to win four of five games to get by Ottawa, something the Senators were not likely to allow given their play in this year's post-season. Buffalo started the game with a 2-0 lead only to see the Senators storm back to take a 3-2 lead. The Sens were crushed when Buffalo tied the game in the dying seconds of the third period to force overtime, but they rebounded when Joe Corvo got a Bobby Baun-type goal in the fifth period of play. Ottawa was going home after winning two road games in a row. The game started out like it would be a Buffalo blowout, though. Thomas Vanek and Jochen Hecht scored in the first six minutes to open a huge 2-0 lead, scoring on two of their first five shots against Ray Emery. Worse for Ottawa, the Sabres were a combined 46-0 in the regular season and playoffs in games they led 2-0. No matter. Ottawa didn't pay attention to statistics, only the scoreboard. The Senators got a huge goal when Daniel Alfredsson scored later in the first, so although they were outshot 15-8, the Sens trailed only 2-1 after the first 20 minutes. The rest of the game belonged to the Sens, who kept chipping away and playing a patient and confident game. They scored the only two goals of the second, both on the power play, to turn the tables on the Sabres and take a 3-2 lead. Mike Fisher scored at 6:08 with Derek Roy in the box for high-sticking and later Wade Redden scored in the final

Antoine Vermette leaps high in the air as Buffalo goalie Ryan Miller blocks a shot in front.

minute during a five-on-three for the Sens on a beautiful one-timer. In the third, they continued to dominate, and Emery was rock solid in goal, but they weren't able to get that insurance goal. In the final minute, Miller went to the bench and Buffalo had six attackers. Tim Connolly took a shot that hit defenceman Wade Redden in front, and the puck came right to Daniel Briere by the right post. He banged it home with just 5.8 seconds left to send the game into overtime. Ottawa still played without fear. The Sens held the edge in play during the fourth period despite having the only penalty to kill off, that to Joe Corvo halfway through. How fitting that the fifth period hero would be Corvo himself. With a faceoff deep in Buffalo territory, Jason Spezza won the draw back to the point. Corvo smacked at the bouncing puck and it dribbled its way crazily past Miller and into the net in fashion similar to Bobby Baun's historic goal in game six of the 1964 Stanley Cup finals. It wasn't pretty, but they don't draw goals, as the expression goes. The Senators won the game and were on their way home with a commanding lead in the series.

Ottawa leads best-of-seven 2-0

The Senators celebrate their overtime win in Buffalo, giving them a 2-0 series lead heading home.

Conference Finals: Ottawa Senators vs. Buffalo Sabres

Game 3
May 14, 2007
Buffalo 0 at **Ottawa** 1

Despite the fact that only one goal was scored, it would be inaccurate to characterize this pivotal game as a goaltenders' battle. That's because Ryan Miller was sensational for Buffalo in stopping 31 of 32 shots while Ottawa's Ray Emery was hardly tested all night. He blocked 15 mostly harmless shots to earn his third shutout of these playoffs on a night when his team was, quite simply, exceptional. It should have been a four- or five-goal win for the Senators but for Miller's play. For the Sabres, though, they returned to their hotel room after this game a downtrodden and confused group. The Senators were simply playing much better, smarter, and more effective hockey. For starters, Buffalo was now 0-for-18 on the power play in this series. Second, and perhaps more important, the Sabres could not match the emotional intensity of Ottawa and couldn't stifle a potent Ottawa offense. The game's only goal

Daniel Alfredsson scores the only goal of the game, taking advantage of a Ryan Miller miscue and pushing the puck into the open net.

came midway through the game on a strange play, Miller's only miscue of the night. Dany Heatley shot the puck wide of the goal, but it caromed hard back off the end boards into Miller's crease. Miller came out to play the puck, but it bounced off his glove and dropped into the blue ice where Daniel Alfredsson gave it a push over the goal line. It was not a goal to describe to his grandchildren, perhaps, but it was the only goal of the game nonetheless. Before and after the goal, Ottawa played no differently. The players kept moving forward, figuring the best defence was to keep the puck in the Buffalo end, and they played impeccably well in their own end. They also managed to stay out of the penalty box, and the few times they were called the penalty killers were, literally, perfect. The Sens outshot Buffalo 32-15, including 10-5 in the third period when the Sabres desperately needed a goal. It never came.

Ottawa leads best-of-seven 3-0

Conference Finals: Ottawa Senators vs. Buffalo Sabres

Derek Roy scores the first goal of the game just nine seconds after the opening faceoff.

Game 4
May 16, 2007
Buffalo 3 at Ottawa 2

Almost, but not quite. Ottawa fell behind 3-0 and then rallied, but came up just short against a proud and talented group of Buffalo Sabres. The win gave the Buffalos slim life heading home for game four, but they still trailed 3-1 in the series. Only twice before had a team ever rallied from 3-0 to win, so odds were clearly not in their favour (the 1942 Toronto Maple Leafs and 1975 New York Islanders did the trick, the Leafs in the finals, the Isles in an earlier round). This time, a great night by goalie Ryan Miller found support from his teammates who finally put some goals on the scoreboard. Miller saved his best for last, maintaining the one-goal lead during a third period the Senators did everything but score. The tone was set from the opening faceoff, though. Buffalo got the puck into the Ottawa end right away, and defenceman Andrej Meszaros went back to get the puck. His outlet pass hit Derek Roy by the net and went to Chris Drury at the blueline. Drury immediately sent it back to Roy, and he chipped the puck over Ray Emery for the goal. It came just nine seconds from the start while fans were still finding their seats and cheering the beginning of the game. Indeed, that was the only

Maxim Afinogenov scores Buffalo's second goal of the game and first power-play goal of the series to give the Sabres a 2-0 lead.

goal of the first period as Ottawa calmed down, but the damage had been done. The Sabres also took the only three penalties of the first, but Ottawa couldn't beat Miller on the power play. The Sabres pulled away with two goals early in the second, again changing the setting from the first three games. Maxim Afinogenov got Buffalo's first power-play goal, that on a five-on-three at 4:32, and then Chris Drury made it 3-0 when his shot from the circle squeaked by Emery. The Sabres now had the lead they wanted, but they still had more than half a game to play. The Senators then started their rally. Dean McAmmond scored at 14:55 and then less than two minutes later Peter Schaefer made it 3-2 on the team's very next shot. That set the stage for a wild third period in which Ottawa held a 15-7 advantage in shots. Try as they might, though, they couldn't beat Miller, even when they had two early power-play chances. The best save was off Joe Corvo when Miller's glove hand bettered a Corvo blast from in close. The Sabres were still alive. The loss ended Ottawa's six-game winning streak, but Ottawa could take comfort that it had not lost back-to-back games since before Christmas.

Ottawa leads best-of-seven 3-1

Game 5

May 19, 2007
Ottawa 3 at Buffalo 2 (OT)

A bounce here or a shot there, and the game and series might have been different. It was a game that both teams had leads in, and lost, and in the end the decisive goal, scored by Daniel Alfredsson, was more pulp fiction than poetry. It was the most evenly-played game of the series, but in the end Ottawa won and advanced to the Stanley Cup finals for the first time in the franchise's history. For Buffalo, it was another conference finals heartbreak. Jochen Hecht scored the game's first goal at 4:30 of the second period after a tense and uneventful opening 20 minutes. The Senators responded with two quick goals late in the period to turn a 1-0 deficit into a 2-1 advantage. Both were scored by the number-one line of Jason Spezza-Dany Heatley-Alfredsson, Heatley getting the tying goal at 15:41 and Spezza putting the Senators out front at 19:21. Playing life-and-death hockey in the final period, the Sabres tied the game at the end of a five-on-three when Maxim Afinogenov surprised Ray Emery on a wraparound. The Sabres dominated the period from start to finish, outshooting Ottawa 11-3, but they couldn't get the winner and the game went to overtime. The deciding score was hardly a classic. Heatley moved the puck to Alfredsson

Jason Spezza scores the go-ahead goal for the Senators to make it 2-1.

The Senators celebrate Daniel Alfredsson's overtime goal which advanced the team to the Stanley Cup finals for the first time in team history.

coming up through centre ice, and as he crossed the blueline he was surrounded by three Buffalo players. Alfredsson let fly a quick wrist shot, and the puck deflected off defenceman Brian Campbell's stick, off the goalpost, and in. Time of the goal was 9:32 of the first overtime. The Ottawa bench emptied, and the Sabres hung their heads in disappointment in front of the home crowd. For the Senators, there could be no more fitting hero. Alfredsson was the only player to have appeared in all of Ottawa's 94 playoff games in the ten years they had made the playoffs, and he had captained the team with pride and dignity. The Senators now boasted a 12-3 playoff record and were the only team to win all series in fewer than six games. The game started out being broadcast in the U.S. by NBC, but when overtime extended the coverage the broadcaster ditched the game for pre-race coverage of the Preakness Stakes, a colossal embarrassment of a decision which deprived many American viewers of the dramatic finish. The overtime was shown only on Versus, a cable channel with a much smaller audience than NBC.

Ottawa wins best-of-seven 4-1

Conference Finals: Ottawa Senators vs. Buffalo Sabres

Stanley Cup Finals
Ottawa Senators vs. Anaheim Ducks

Mike Comrie looks to be knocking the puck in the net but Mike Fisher's shot goes in on its own to give Ottawa the early 1-0 lead in game one of the Stanley Cup finals.

Game 1

May 28, 2007
Ottawa 2 at Anaheim 3

The storylines to this series before game one faceoff were many: Could Ottawa handle playing a physical game against the tough Ducks? Could Anaheim's big three on defence—Scott Niedermayer, Chris Pronger, Francois Beauchemin—handle the big Ottawa trio of Dany Heatley-Jason Spezza-Daniel Alfredsson? Would Ray Emery play as well as J-S Giguere in goal? Would special teams be the decisive factor? Could Ottawa play as well in the finals, with so little experience, against a Ducks team that had been to the finals three years earlier? Some of these questions were answered after game one, a game in which Ottawa twice had the lead but failed to hold, while others were not so easily understood.

The Senators struck first and early, getting a lucky goal at just 1:38. With Scott Niedermayer in the penalty box serving a high-sticking penalty, Mike Fisher took a routine shot that caught Giguere by surprise. The goalie managed only to get a glove on the puck, and the disc bounced high in the air, landing on the goal line and trickling into the net before Sean O'Donnell could bat it out of harm's way. It was a big goal for the

Senators as they were 8-0 during the 2007 playoffs when they scored first. The Ducks tied the game midway through the period, however, thanks to some great puck pressure on the Ottawa defence. They got the puck in deep and then Drew Miller hit Chris Phillips as he got rid of the puck in his end, forcing a turnover. Teemu Selanne was right there to claim the loose puck. Selanne made a gorgeous little drop pass to Andy MacDonald who ripped a hard shot over the glove of Emery to tie the score, 1-1. The Senators took the lead early in the second period on another power play. This time, Redden's point shot found the top corner over Giguere's shoulder on a play that was scrambly at best on Anaheim's part. Joe Corvo had hit the post with a shot, and in trying to recover Giguere lost his stick when he got tangled up with defenceman Niedermayer. The Sens moved the puck around quickly as the Ducks tried to get the stick back to their goalie, and as this was going on Redden blasted a hard shot into the net. Ottawa, which had gone 0-for-16 in the last three games of the Buffalo series with the extra man, now had two power-play goals in the first half of game one of the finals. The Sens then had a great chance to break the game wide open when they had a lengthy five-on-three, but the Ducks held their ground and kept it a 2-1 game after 40 minutes. This proved to be a turning point as Anaheim scored the only two goals of the final period. On the tying goal, Ryan Getzlaf made a brilliant rush. Streaking down the right wing, the right-hand shot faked as if he were going to skate around the net. Instead, he quickly shifted the puck to his backhand and made a great shot along the ice to the far side, fooling Emery. Travis Moen got the winning goal with just 2:51 left in regulation time. He found a loose puck in the slot and drilled a shot past a helpless Emery to give the Ducks a win in the opening game of the finals.

Anaheim leads best-of-seven 1-0.

Travis Moen's third-period shot eludes Ray Emery and gives Anaheim a 3-2 win in game one.

Game 2

May 30, 2007
Ottawa 0 at Anaheim 1

The Senators had lost only three games all playoffs, and they followed each loss with a win. In fact, the last time the Senators lost two games in a row was before Christmas. But one shot, one goal, late in the third period was all that Anaheim needed this night. Samuel Pahlsson was the hero, spoiling a great performance by Ottawa goalie Ray Emery. Coach Bryan Murray made only one change to his lineup for this important game, taking Patrick Eaves out of the lineup and inserting Oleg Saprykin in his place. A more superficial change came on the first two shifts when Murray broke up his top line of Dany Heatley-Jason Spezza-Daniel Alfredsson, but this lasted only a few minutes. Unlike game one, this started with Anaheim domination of puck possession while the Senators countered with several major-league bodychecks to assert the physical game. The Ducks had a couple of very effective power plays, but Emery was sharp in the Ottawa net. By the midway point of the first period, shots were 10-1 Anaheim, but the game was still scoreless. Ottawa had a great chance later in the period with a five-on-three for 68 seconds, but despite several incredible scoring chances the team failed to get that big first goal. Anaheim dominated the second period to such an extent that were it not for Emery, the game would have been as good as over. The Ducks proved the quicker team all period, getting to loose pucks first, forcing turnovers in the Ottawa end, and creating scoring chances through hard work. Emery made several great saves, and time and again the Ducks brought the puck out from behind the end red line and tried to stuff the puck in, to no avail. Shots were 14-4 for the Ducks, a count that fairly reflected the edge in play during the middle 20 minutes. The third period was more of the same from Anaheim.

Mike Fisher (left) and Anton Volchenkov team up to check Corey Perry.

Samuel Pahlsson's quick shot beats Emery to the far side late in game two, the only goal of the game.

The Ducks came out putting pressure on the puck carrier deep in the Ottawa end, forcing turnovers and creating chances. Yet Ottawa played disciplined hockey inside its own blueline, and the longer the game remained scoreless the greater the chances of the Senators taking the game to overtime seemed. A turnover at the Anaheim blueline changed that, though. Spezza and Heatley got crossed up carrying the puck over the Anaheim line, and Pahlsson picked up the loose puck and stormed down the right wing, his off wing. His speed put defenceman Joe Corvo on the defensive, and when Pahlsson stopped quickly at the faceoff dot, Corvo could only spin and hope to catch a piece of him. Pahlsson fired a quick shot between Corvo's legs, off the far post, and past a surprised Emery for the first and only goal of the game at 14:15 of the third period. Ottawa stormed the net of J-S Giguere in the dying minutes, but the scoring touch simply wasn't there. Peter Schaefer had a wide open net on one flurry but missed the target, and the Ducks' defencemen blocked several shots that might have been dangerous had they reached the net. The better team won this game, and Ottawa was now in a serious hole. Yes, the Senators were going home for two games, but they were trailing by 2-0 in the series as well. They could ill afford to lose the next game.

Anaheim leads best-of-seven 2-0

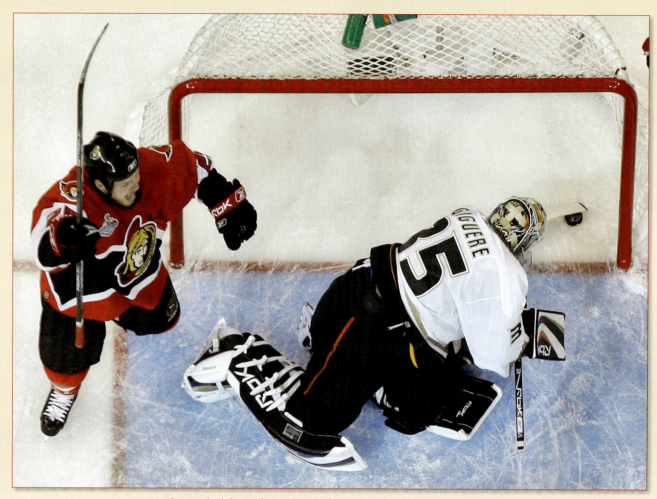

Chris Neil celebrates his goal in the first period that ties the game at 1-1.

Game 3

June 2, 2007

Anaheim 3 at **Ottawa** 5

Although Anaheim was only half way to its goal, this was a game Ottawa had to win. If the Sens lost, they would be trailing 3-0 in the series, and only once in 65 years of best-of-seven finals has a team rallied from down three games to win, that the Leafs from 1945. Indeed, Ottawa responded with a gritty effort, and led by Chris Kelly, Chris Neil and Mike Fisher, the team rallied three times to win 5-3. The stars for Anaheim so far in this series had been the checking line of Sami Pahlsson-Travis Moen-Rob Niedermayer, but playing in Ottawa allowed Sens coach Bryan Murray to get his three big scorers away from the checkers by virtue of having last line change at stoppages. Still, the Sens started out looking nervous, despite the support from the red-clad Scotiabank Place crowd. Anaheim drew first blood on an early power play, scoring a goal that should never have happened. Ray Emery played the puck along the boards to Mike Fisher, but he was slow in turning and firing it out and was checked off the puck. Teemu Selanne wound up with it behind the net, and as he circled he saw Andy McDonald in the slot. McDonald's quick one-timer beat Emery to the short side, and it looked as though the Ducks were picking up from where they left off in the third period of game two when the Ducks were so successful. For most of the rest of the period the Sens could do little as passes misfired and the Ducks played simple and effective defence. Late in the period, though, the big three of Jason Spezza-Dany-Heatley-Daniel Alfredsson has an exceptional shift, controlling the puck for more than a minute in the Anaheim end. Although they didn't score, their replacements did. Chris Neil worked hard to create a turnover just inside the Ducks' blueline, and Chris Kelly skated along the outside with the puck. He spotted Neil roaring to the net and made the pass, and Neil redirected it quickly to the far side past J-S Giguere to tie the game. It was Ottawa's first goal in more

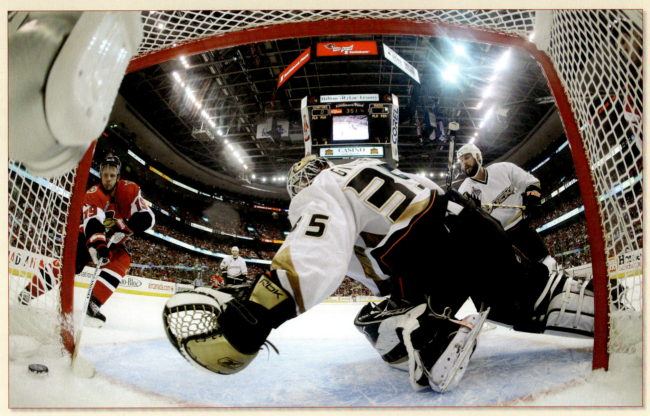

J-S Giguere can't stop the puck before it goes in.

than five periods and gave the team much needed life. The Sens didn't come out flying to start the second, but the middle period turned out to be the most Ottawa-style period of the series so far. There were plenty of goals and the Sens finally found their skating legs and pressured the Anaheim defencemen for the first time. It was the Ducks, though, that went ahead 2-1 early on a weak goal allowed by Emery. Corey Perry skated out from the corner boards and simply slid the puck through the goalie's legs at 5:20. Just 27 seconds later, though, Ottawa tied the score after Mike Fisher beat Sami Pahlsson on a faceoff deep in the Anaheim end. The puck went back to Anton Volchenkov at the point, and his shot was deflected by Fisher over the shoulder of Giguere. A few minutes later, the Ducks went ahead for a third time, again on a weak play by Emery.

He stopped an easy shot from Dustin Penner but coughed up a generous rebound, and Ryan Getzlaf blasted it home from in close to make it 3-2 Ducks. Then the Sens went to work. They earned back-to-back power-play chances, and midway through the second one got a lucky goal. A point shot bounced off Alfredsson's skate and in, and after a lengthy video review the goal was allowed. It came at 16:14 and was Ottawa's first power-play goal on home ice in its last 22 opportunities. The Sens took the lead for the first time when Oleg Saprykin got to a loose puck first and passed it to Dean McAmmond. He centred the puck quickly in the slot, but Chris Pronger, trying to clear it, tipped it into his own goal at 18:34. After a wild and strange period, the Sens headed to the dressing room with a 4-3 lead after 40 minutes. The question that remained was whether

Ottawa could build on or at least hold this lead through the final 20 minutes of intense hockey. The answer was a resounding yes, thanks in part to Pronger again. Early in the third, he delivered a vicious elbow to Dean McAmmond after the Ottawa forward had taken a shot, an infraction that went unpunished. On the next shift, a melee ensued involving all players, and the Sens were playing as a team with a cause. The Sens got the only goal of the period thanks to more hard work in the corners. Chris Kelly tied up his man, and Antoine Vermette came in and took the puck behind the net. He saw Volchenkov move into the slot, and the pass and shot were perfect. The Sens played with controlled emotion the rest of the way, and got themselves back into the series.

Anaheim leads best-of-seven 2-1

Stanley Cup Finals: Ottawa Senators vs. Anaheim Ducks

Game 4
June 4, 2007
Anaheim 3 at Ottawa 2

The pre-game favourites for game four must have been the Senators on three counts: they were playing at home; they had won the last game; they were playing an Anaheim team that was without defenceman Chris Pronger who was suspended for one game for his vicious elbow to the head of Dean McAmmond two nights earlier. On that last point, however, there was a real danger of the Senators becoming over-confident.

J-S Giguere can't squeeze his arm to his side quickly enough as Daniel Alfredsson's shot beats him in the final second of the first period to give Ottawa a 1-0 lead.

When Pronger sat out a game the previous series for a dirty hit on Niklas Lidstrom of Detroit, the Ducks won the game 5-3. As it turned out, a third-period goal from Dustin Penner proved the difference, and the Ducks won again without Pronger. It was a tough loss for the Senators to absorb. The Senators had two early power-play chances to open the scoring, but the first was ineffective and the second, while replete with chances, also yielded nothing. Nonetheless, the Senators were skating and hitting and getting to loose pucks, and by the midway point of the first they were outshooting Anaheim, 9-0. J-S Giguere was strong in goal for the Ducks, but the Sens had trouble finishing what they started. In fact, the best chance of the first half came from Corey Perry who hit the crossbar skating down the left wing on a two-on-one. The only goal of the period came in the dying seconds with the Senators on another power play. Mike Fisher worked the puck free deep in the Anaheim end and passed it to Peter Schaefer behind the goal. He immediately put it out front to Daniel Alferedsson, and his quick shot snuck under the blocking arm of Giguere with less than one second left on the clock. The Senators had a critical 1-0 lead after 20 minutes in a period they outshot Anaheim, 13-2. The second period was just as lop-sided, but the other way. The Ducks had two early power plays, and they cashed in just as the second expired. Andy McDonald hit the crossbar early on, but he made no mistake after getting the puck in front. He held onto it and moved to the side, and Emery slid well out of position. McDonald merely slid the puck in the open side at 10:06 to make it 1-1. Exactly 60 seconds later, he gave the Ducks the lead. Rob Niedermayer made a beautiful pass to him in the centre-ice area, and then McDonald deked Anton Volchenkov badly and

J-S Giguere can't stop the puck before it goes in.

slide the puck between Emery's legs as the goalie again slid way out of position. The goal, McDonald's ninth of the playoffs, stunned the crowd, and Ottawa was reeling. Late in the period, though, in a flash, the Senators tied the game. Jason Spezza had the puck along the boards in the Anaheim end and passed to the side of the net to Patrick Eaves. He had a mini-two-on-one with Dany Heatley who moved quickly to the front of the net. Eaves made a perfect pass, and Heatley converted it with an equally perfect shot at 18:00 to make it a 2-2 game with one period left to play. Unfortunately for the Sens, Anaheim came out and played with more tenacity, showing, quite simply, a greater desire to win. The Ducks got the break they needed early on when Teemu Selanne and Penner came in on a confused-looking two-on-two, but Selanne quickly got by Wade Redden and Penner drove to the net. Selanne's pass eluded a sprawling Anton Volchenkov, and Penner redirected the puck into the open net as Emery overplayed the shooter. The Sens generated only limited offense the rest of the game, and Anaheim was now heading home for game five with a chance to close out the series.

Anaheim leads best-of-seven 3-1.

Stanley Cup Finals: Ottawa Senators vs. Anaheim Ducks

Game 5

June 6, 2007
Ottawa 2 at Anaheim 6

The Stanley Cup was in the building. So, too, was Chris Pronger, back on the Anaheim blueline after serving a one-game suspension. Ric Jackman was out for the Ducks and Chris Kunitz was in. For the Senators, coach Bryan Murray made no changes from his game four lineup, hoping the same players could skate their way into a game six. They couldn't. The things that got the Sens this far were the reasons they couldn't extend the series or win the Cup. Goalie Ray Emery was weak, and the scorers, notably Jason Spezza and Dany Heatley, failed to score. The referees were the stars of the first period, calling six minors, three first to Ottawa, then three to the Ducks, all of which were marginal infractions at best. The Ducks had an early five-on-three and scored the game's first goal toward the end of the second of the consecutive power plays. Andy McDonald had the puck along the boards to Ray Emery's left, and as McDonald threw a pass in front it banked off the skate of Wade Redden and slid between the goalie's pads at 3:41. This woeful start had the Sens on their heels for much of the rest of the period, and even with the man advantage Ottawa could not gain puck possession inside the Anaheim blueline. Time and again the Sens shot the puck in, and almost every time the Ducks cleared it right back out. Late in the period, seconds after the expiration of an Anaheim penalty, the Ducks went up by two goals. Rob Niedermayer carried the puck down the right side and cut in on goal while forward Mike Comrie tried to block his path. Niedermayer was not to be outmuscled, and his simple backhand shot beat Emery under his blocking arm at 17:41. It was another weak goal for Emery in this series, and it gave the home

Rob Niedermayer puts the finishing touches on a great rush, beating Ray Emery with a backhand under the blocking arm.

side a huge 2-0 lead after one period. Try as the Sens might to get back into the game, bad luck and poor play scuppered their efforts. Daniel Alfredsson had his best period of the playoffs in the second, scoring two beautiful and important goals, only to see each wiped out by an Anaheim score. On the first, he dug the puck free along the boards, fed the puck to Mike Fisher, and went to the slot. Fisher's pass was deftly deflected by Peter Schaefer right to Alfredsson, and he made a great shot to the top corner to make it 2-1 at 9:27. Later in the period, though, Chris Phillips and Emery combined for one of the worst goals in Cup finals history. Emery left an Anaheim dump-in of the puck behind his goal, and Phillips pushed the puck up a few feet. It got caught in Emery's skates, and he unwittingly pushed it into the net. It was a crushing goal, but it was offset by a tremendous individual effort by the captain, Alfredsson. On an Anaheim power play, he stole the puck from Ryan Getzlaf at the Ottawa blueline and went in on goal, fighting off Getzlaf the whole way. Alfredsson ripped a shot high to the short side to make it a 3-2 game at 17:38, and it looked like the Sens had life again. But just 50 seconds later, on the same man advantage, Francois Beauchemin's point shot deflected in front off Volchenkov and past Emery to restore Anaheim's two-goal lead after 40 minutes. The Ducks were not going to blow a two-goal lead when they were just 20 minutes from winning the Stanley Cup. They got a break early in the third when Emery gave the puck to Scott Niedermayer on a clearing attempt, and his long shot was tipped by Travis Moen past the goalie to make it 5-2 and seal the victory. Things went so wrong for the Sens this night that even when Antoine Vermette was awarded a penalty shot, he lost control of the puck and didn't even get a shot on goal. Corey Perry scored the final goal after a bad giveaway by Alfredsson, and for the first time in Cup history the trophy was won by a California team. Scott Niedermayer hoisted the Cup as Anaheim captain, and he took home the Conn Smythe Trophy as well for his outstanding playoff performance. For the Sens, it was the end of their finest season ever, a season to build on for another run at the Cup in 2008.

Anaheim wins best-of-seven 4-1.

Anaheim captain Scott Niedermayer hoists the Cup after the Ducks beat Ottawa 6-2 in the deciding game.

Stanley Cup Finals: Ottawa Senators vs. Anaheim Ducks

THE ORIGINAL SENATORS:
Previous appearances in the playoffs
1918–1934

1917-18 DNQ

1918-19 NHL Finals Ottawa vs. Montreal Canadiens
February 22 Ottawa 4 at Canadiens 8
February 27 Canadiens 5 at Ottawa 3
March 1 Ottawa 3 at Canadiens 6
March 3 Canadiens 3 at Ottawa 6
March 6 Ottawa 2 at Canadiens 4
Canadiens won best-of-seven 4-1 to advance to Stanley Cup finals

1919-20 Stanley Cup Finals Ottawa vs. Seattle Metropolitans
March 22 Seattle 2 at Ottawa 3
March 24 Seattle 0 at Ottawa 3 [Benedict]
March 27 Seattle 3 at Ottawa 1
March 30 Seattle 5 Ottawa 2 (played at Toronto)
April 1 Ottawa 6 Seattle 1 (played at Toronto)
Ottawa won Stanley Cup best-of-five 3-2

1920-21 NHL Finals Ottawa vs. Toronto St. Pats
March 10 Toronto 0 at Ottawa 5 [Benedict]
March 15 Ottawa 2 at Toronto 0 [Benedict]
Ottawa won two-game total-goals series 7-0 to advance to Stanley Cup finals

Stanley Cup Finals Ottawa vs. Vancouver Millionaires
March 21 Ottawa 1 at Vancouver 3
March 24 Ottawa 4 at Vancouver 3
March 28 Ottawa 3 at Vancouver 2
March 31 Ottawa 2 at Vancouver 3
April 4 Ottawa 2 at Vancouver 1
Ottawa won Stanley Cup best-of-five 3-2

1921-22 NHL Finals Ottawa vs. Toronto St. Pats
March 11 Ottawa 4 at Toronto 5
March 13 Toronto 0 at Ottawa 0 [Roach/Benedict]
Toronto won two-game total-goals series 5-4 to advance to Stanley Cup finals

1922-23 NHL Finals Ottawa vs. Montreal Canadiens
March 7 Ottawa 2 at Canadiens 0 [Benedict]
March 9 Canadiens 2 at Ottawa 1
Ottawa won two-game total-goals series 3-2 to advance to Stanley Cup playoffs

Stanley Cup Playoffs Ottawa vs. Vancouver Millionaires
March 16 Ottawa 1 at Vancouver 0 [Benedict]
March 19 Ottawa 1 at Vancouver 4
March 23 Ottawa 3 at Vancouver 2
March 26 Ottawa 5 at Vancouver 1
Ottawa won best-of-five semi-finals 3-1
Stanley Cup Finals Ottawa vs. Edmonton Eskimos
March 29 Ottawa 2 Edmonton 1 (Cy Denney 2:08 OT)
March 31 Ottawa 1 Edmonton 0 [Benedict]
Ottawa won Stanley Cup best-of-three 2-0

1923-24 NHL Finals Ottawa vs. Montreal Canadiens
March 8 Ottawa 0 at Canadiens 1 [Vezina]
March 11 Canadiens 4 at Ottawa 2
Canadiens won two-game total-goals series 5-2

1924-25 DNQ

1925-26 DNQ

1926-27 Semi-finals Ottawa vs. Montreal Canadiens
April 2 Ottawa 4 at Canadiens 0 [Connell]
April 4 Canadiens 1 at Ottawa 1
Ottawa won best-of-two total-goals series 5-1

Stanley Cup Finals Ottawa vs. Boston Bruins
April 7 Ottawa 0 at Boston 0 [Connell/Winkler]
April 9 Ottawa 3 at Boston 1
April 11 Boston 1 at Ottawa 1
April 13 Boston 1 at Ottawa 3
Ottawa won Stanley Cup best-of-five 2-0-2

1927-28 Quarter-finals Ottawa vs. Montreal Maroons
March 27 Maroons 1 at Ottawa 0 [Benedict]
March 29 Ottawa 1 at Maroons 2
Maroons won best-of-two total-goals series 3-1

1928-29 DNQ

1929-30 Quarter-finals Ottawa vs. New York Rangers
March 20 Rangers 1 at Ottawa 1
March 23 Ottawa 2 at Rangers 5
Rangers won best-of-two total-goals series 6-3

1930-31 DNQ

1931-32 DNQ

1932-33 DNQ

1933-34 DNQ

THE MODERN SENATORS:
Previous appearances in the playoffs
1992–2006

1996-97
April 17   Ottawa 1 at Buffalo 3
April 19   Ottawa 3 at Buffalo 1
April 21   Buffalo 3 at Ottawa 2
April 23   Buffalo 0 at Ottawa 1 (Alfredsson 2:34 OT) [Tugnutt]
April 25   Ottawa 4 at Buffalo 1
April 27   Buffalo 3 at Ottawa 0 [Shields]
April 29   Ottawa 2 at Buffalo 3 (Plante 5:24 OT)
Buffalo won best-of-seven 4-3

1997-98
April 22   Ottawa 2 at New Jersey 1 (Gardiner 5:58 OT)
April 24   Ottawa 1 at New Jersey 3
April 26   New Jersey 1 at Ottawa 2 (Yashin 2:47 OT)
April 28   New Jersey 3 at Ottawa 4
April 30   Ottawa 1 at New Jersey 3
May 2   New Jersey 1 at Ottawa 4
Ottawa won best-of-seven 4-2

May 7   Ottawa 2 at Washington 4
May 9   Ottawa 1 at Washington 6
May 11   Washington 3 at Ottawa 4
May 13   Washington 2 at Ottawa 0 [Kolzig]
May 15   Ottawa 0 at Washington 3 [Kolzig]
Washington won best-of-seven 4-1

1998-99
April 21   Buffalo 2 at Ottawa 1
April 23   Buffalo 3 at Ottawa 2 (Satan 30:35 OT)
April 25   Ottawa 0 at Buffalo 3 [Hasek]
April 27   Ottawa 3 at Buffalo 4
Buffalo won best-of-seven 4-0

1999-2000
April 12   Ottawa 0 at Toronto 2 [Joseph]
April 15   Ottawa 1 at Toronto 5
April 17   Toronto 3 at Ottawa 4
April 19   Toronto 1 at Ottawa 2
April 22   Ottawa 1 at Toronto 2 (Thomas 14:47 OT)
April 24   Toronto 4 at Ottawa 2
Toronto won best-of-seven 4-2

2000-01
April 13   Toronto 1 at Ottawa 0 (Sundin 10:49 OT) [Joseph]
April 14   Toronto 3 at Ottawa 0 [Joseph]
April 16   Ottawa 2 at Toronto 3 (Cross 2:16 OT)
April 18   Ottawa 1 at Toronto 3
Toronto won best-of-seven 4-0

2001-02
Apr 17   Ottawa 0 at Philadelphia 1 (Fedotenko 7:47 OT) [Cechmanek]
Apr 20   Ottawa 3 at Philadelphia 0 [Lalime]
Apr 22   Philadelphia 0 at Ottawa 3 [Lalime]
Apr 24   Philadelphia 0 at Ottawa 3 [Lalime]
Apr 26   Ottawa 2 at Philadelphia 1 (Havlat 7:33 OT)
Ottawa won best-of-seven 4-1

May 2   Ottawa 5 at Toronto 0 [Lalime]
May 4   Ottawa 2 at Toronto 3 (Roberts 44:30 OT)
May 6   Toronto 2 at Ottawa 3
May 8   Toronto 2 at Ottawa 1
May 10   Ottawa 4 at Toronto 2
May 12   Toronto 4 at Ottawa 3
May 14   Ottawa 0 at Toronto 3 [Joseph]
Toronto won best-of-seven 4-3

2002-03
April 9   Islanders 3 at Ottawa 0 [Snow]
April 12   Islanders 0 at Ottawa 3 [Lalime]
April 14   Ottawa 3 at Islanders 2 (White 22:25 OT)
April 16   Ottawa 3 at Islanders 1
April 17   Islanders 1 at Ottawa 4
Ottawa won best-of-seven 4-1

April 25   Philadelphia 2 at Ottawa 4
April 27   Philadelphia 2 at Ottawa 0 [Cechmanek]
April 29   Ottawa 3 at Philadelphia 2 (Redden 6:43 OT)
May 1   Ottawa 0 at Philadelphia 1 (Handzus 17:06 1st) [Cechmanek]
May 3   Philadelphia 2 at Ottawa 5
May 5   Ottawa 5 at Philadelphia 1
Ottawa won best-of-seven 4-2

May 10   New Jersey 2 at Ottawa 3 (Van Allen 3:08 OT)
May 13   New Jersey 4 at Ottawa 1
May 15   Ottawa 0 at New Jersey 1 (Brylin 1st) [Brodeur]
May 17   Ottawa 2 at New Jersey 5
May 19   New Jersey 1 at Ottawa 3
May 21   Ottawa 2 at New Jersey 1 (Phillips 15:51 OT)
May 23   New Jersey 3 at Ottawa 2
New Jersey won best-of-seven 4-3

2003-04
April 8   Ottawa 4 at Toronto 2
April 10   Ottawa 0 at Toronto 2 [Belfour]
April 12   Toronto 2 at Ottawa 0 [Belfour]
April 14   Toronto 1 at Ottawa 4
April 16   Ottawa 0 at Toronto 2 [Belfour]
April 18   Toronto 1 at Ottawa 2 (Fisher 21:47 OT)
April 20   Ottawa 1 at Toronto 4
Toronto won best-of-seven 4-3

2005-06
April 21   Tampa Bay 1 at Ottawa 4
April 23   Tampa Bay 4 at Ottawa 3
April 25   Ottawa 8 at Tampa Bay 4
April 27   Ottawa 5 at Tampa Bay 2
April 29   Tampa Bay 2 at Ottawa 3
Ottawa won best-of-seven 4-1

May 5   Buffalo 7 at Ottawa 6 (Drury 0:18 OT)
May 8   Buffalo 2 at Ottawa 1
May 10   Ottawa 2 at Buffalo 3 (Dumont 5:05 OT)
May 11   Ottawa 2 at Buffalo 1
May 13   Buffalo 3 at Ottawa 2 (Pominville 2:26 OT)
Buffalo won best-of-seven 4-1

All-Time Playoff Record

(bold indicates won Stanley Cup)

	GP	W	L	T	GF	GA
1917-18	DNQ					
1918-19	5	1	4	0	18	26
1919-20	5	3	2	0	15	11
1920-21	7	5	2	0	19	12
1921-22	2	0	1	1	4	5
1922-23	8	6	2	0	16	10
1923-24	2	0	2	0	2	5
1924-25	DNQ					
1925-26	DNQ					
1926-27	6	3	0	3	12	4
1927-28	2	0	2	0	1	3
1928-29	DNQ					
1929-30	2	0	1	1	3	6
1930-31	DNQ					
1931-32	DNQ					
1932-33	DNQ					
1933-34	DNQ					
Totals	**39**	**18**	**16**	**5**	**90**	**82**

	GP	W	L	GF	GA
1992-93	DNQ				
1993-94	DNQ				
1994-95	DNQ				
1995-96	DNQ				
1996-97	7	3	4	13	14
1997-98	11	5	6	21	30
1998-99	4	0	4	6	12
1999-2000	6	2	4	10	17
2000-01	4	0	4	3	10
2001-02	12	7	5	29	18
2002-03	18	11	7	43	34
2003-04	7	3	4	11	14
2004-05	SEASON CANCELLED				
2005-06	10	5	5	36	29
Totals	**79**	**36**	**43**	**172**	**178**

All-Time Draft Choices

1992
2	Alexei Yashin
25	Chad Penney
50	Patrick Traverse
73	Radek Hamr
98	Daniel Guerard
121	Alan Sinclair
146	Jaroslav Miklenda
169	Jay Kenney
194	Claude Savoie
217	Jake Grimes
242	Tomas Jelinek
264	Petter Ronnqvist

1993
1	Alexander Daigle
27	Radim Bicanek
53	Patrick Charbonneau
91	Cosmo Dupaul
131	Rick Bodkin
157	Sergei Polischuk
183	Jason Disher
209	Toby Kvalevog
227	Pavol Demitra
235	Rick Schuhwerk

1994
3	Radek Bonk
29	Stanislav Neckar
81	Bryan Masotta
131	Mike Gaffney
133	Daniel Alfredsson
159	Doug Sproule
210	Frederic Cassivi
211	Danny Dupont
237	Steve MacKinnon
274	Antti Tormanen

1995
1	Bryan Berard
27	Marc Moro
53	Brad Larsen
89	Kevin Bolibruck
103	Kevin Boyd
131	David Hruska
183	Kaj Linna
184	Ray Schultz
231	Erik Kaminski

1996
1	Chris Phillips
81	Antti-Jussi Niemi
136	Andreas Dackell
163	Francois Hardy
212	Erich Goldmann
216	Ivan Ciernik
239	Sami Salo

1997
12	Marian Hossa
58	Jani Hurme
66	Josh Langfeld
119	Magnus Arvedson
146	Jeff Sullivan
173	Robin Bacul
203	Nick Gillis
229	Karel Rachunek

1998
15	Mathieu Chouinard
44	Mike Fisher
58	Chris Bala
74	Julien Vauclair
101	Petr Schastlivy
130	Gavin McLeod
161	Chris Neil
188	Michel Periard
223	Sergei Verenikin
246	Rastislav Pavlikosky

1999
26	Martin Havlat
48	Simon Lajeunesse
62	Teemu Sainomaa
94	Chris Kelly
154	Andrew Ianiero
164	Martin Prusek
201	Mikko Ruutu
209	Layne Ulmer
213	Alexandre Giroux
269	Konstantin Korovikov

2000
21	Anton Volchenkov
45	Mathieu Chouinard
55	Antoine Vermette
87	Jan Bohac
122	Derrick Byfuglien
156	Greg Zanon
157	Grant Potulny
158	Sean Connolly
188	Jason Maleyko
283	James Demone

2001
2	Jason Spezza
23	Tim Gleason
81	Neil Komadoski
99	Ray Emery
127	Christoph Schubert
162	Stefan Schauer
193	Brooks Laich
218	Jan Platil
223	Brandon Bochenski
235	Neil Petruic
256	Gregg Johnson
286	Toni Dahlman

2002
16	Jakub Klepis
47	Alexei Kaigorodov
75	Arttu Luttinen
113	Scott Dobben
125	Johan Bjork
150	Brock Hooton
246	Josef Vavra
276	Vitali Atyushov

2003
29	Patrick Eaves
67	Igor Mirnov
100	Philippe Seydoux
135	Mattais Karlsson
142	Tim Cook
166	Sergei Gimayev
228	Will Colbert
260	Ossi Louhivaara
291	Brian Elliott

2004
23	Andrej Meszaros
58	Kirill Lyamin
77	Shawn Weller
87	Peter Regin
89	Jeff Glass
122	Alexander Nikulin
141	Jim McKenzie
156	Roman Wick
219	Joe Cooper
251	Matthew McIlvane
284	John Wikner

2005
9	Brian Lee
70	Vitali Anikeyenko
95	Cody Bass
98	Ilya Zubov
115	Janne Kolehmainen
136	Tomas Kudelka
186	Dmitri Megalinsky
204	Colin Greening

2006
28	Nick Foligno
68	Eric Gryba
91	Kaspars Daugavins
121	Pierre-Luc Lessard
151	Ryan Daniels
181	Kevin Koopman
211	Erik Condra

The Ottawa Silver Seven

At first, they were called the Ottawa Hockey Club, but in the early years of the 1900s the team was so magnificent it earned the nickname Silver Seven (referring to seven players on a team). From 1902 to 1906, the Silver Seven were virtually unbeatable, winning the Stanley Cup every season and staring down all challenges successfully. The 1903 team first defeated the Montreal Victorias 9-1 in the two-game, total-goals series and then in a best-of-three challenge they downed the Rat Portage Thistles 6-2 and 4-2 to win their first Stanley Cup.

The team included Percy Sims, the Gilmour brothers—Dave, Billy, Suddy—Harry Westwick, "One-Eyed" Frank McGee, Fred Wood, Art Fraser, Charles Spittal, captain Harvey Pulford, Art Moore, and goalie Bouse Hutton. Alf Smith was the coach.

The next year, the Silver Seven earned an unprecedented series of wins. By virtue of wining the league title again, it didn't have to go to a playoffs, but the team won four successive challenges from the Winnipeg Rowing Club (2-1 in the best-of-three), Toronto Marlboros (2-0 in the best-of-three), Montreal Wanderers, and a team from Brandon (2-0 in the best-of-three). They tied the Wanderers 5-5, but their opponents refused to play the final two games in Ottawa and were disqualified. The core of the Ottawa team was the same as the previous year.

In 1905, the Silver Seven won an historic challenge from Dawson City, Yukon. Ottawa won the first game 9-2, but it was the second of these which has gone down in history as something almost mythical. Frank McGee scored 14 goals in the team's 23-2 win, a Stanley Cup record that will surely stand forever. The team then withstood another challenge from Rat Portage to end a third season as Cup champions.

The Silver Seven remained champions for a fourth year in 1906 after overpowering two more challenges. The first came from Queen's University in Kingston, Ontario, by two one-sided scores, 16-7 and 12-7. The second came against a team from Smiths Falls, Ontario, Ottawa winning the best-of-three by 6-5 and 8-2. The reign ended on March 17, 1906, when the Montreal Wanderers won a two-game, total-goals series 12-10 in one of the most dramatic showdowns ever. Montreal won the first game 9-1, and Cup victory seemed easily assured. But in the second game, Ottawa poured in goal after goal, and only a late score from the Wanderers averted embarrassment as Ottawa won, 9-3.

The Senators won two more pre-NHL Stanley Cups, in 1909 and 1911. The former included Marty Walsh, Edgar Dey, goalie Percy LeSueur, and Fred Lake. The 1911 win was the result of finishing first in the NHA (National Hockey Association) standings and then winning two more challenges. Ottawa beat Galt 7-4 and three days later beat Port Arthur, 14-4. They were no longer called the Silver Seven then but went by the name Senators.

The Stanley Cup champion Ottawa Senators of 1909.

The Original Ottawa Senators

Members of the Hockey Hall of Fame who played for the Original Senators:

Jack Adams, Clint Benedict, Frank Boucher, Punch Broadbent, Harry Cameron, King Clancy, Sprague Cleghorn, Alec Connell, Rusty Crawford, Jack Darragh, Cy Denneny, Bill Durnan, Eddie Gerard, Billy Gilmour, Syd Howe, Harry Hyland, Percy LeSueur, Frank McGee, Frank Nighbor, Tommy Phillips, Harvey Pulford, Art Ross, Alf Smith, Hooley Smith, Bruce Stuart, Cyclone Taylor, Marty Walsh, Cooney Weiland, Harry Westwick

Stanley Cup Champions:

1919-20 Cy Denneny, Punch Broadbent, Frank Nighbor, Sprague Cleghorn, Clint Benedict, Eddie Gerard, Horace Merrill, George Boucher, Jack Darragh, Morley Bruce, Lack MacKell, Jack Darragh, coach Pete Green

1920-21 Cy Denneny, Punch Broadbent, Frank Nighbor, Sprague Cleghorn, Clint Benedict, Eddie Gerard, Leth Graham, George Boucher, Jack Darragh, Morley Bruce, Jack MacKell, Jack Darragh, coach Pete Green

1922-23 Lionel Hitchman, King Clancy, Harry Helman, Frank Nighbor, Clint Benedict, George Boucher, Jack Darragh, Eddie Gerard, Cy Denneny, Punch Broadbent, coach Pete Green

1926-27 King Clancy, Alec Connell, George Boucher, Ed Gorman, Alex Smith, Frank Finnigan, Hec Kilrea, Hooley Smith, Cy Denneny, Frank Nighbor, Jack Adams, Milt Halliday, coach Dave Gill

The 1927 Stanley Cup parade makes its way through downtown Ottawa as each player travelled the route in his own car.

Tribute to Frank Finnigan

A member of the original Ottawa Senators for ten years, Finnigan rose to prominence again in 1990 as Ottawa's bid to win an expansion franchise intensified. The last surviving member of the 1927 Stanley Cup champions, he scored the last goal in the history of the original Ottawa Senators, on March 15, 1934. Finnigan was part of the promotional team that pitched the NHL on the virtues of Canada's capital city, and after the successful efforts he was set to drop the puck at the home opener in 1992. Unfortunately, he died on December 25, 1991 at age 90, but his number 8 was retired by the team on October 8, 1992. It hangs in the rafters to this day as testament both to his original contributions and to his more recent efforts on behalf of the city and team.

Frank Finnegan was one of the early greats for the Senators.

The Modern Senators

Hockey Hall of Fame
Roger Neilson

Trophy Winners
Jack Adams Award
Jacques Martin (1998-99)

Calder Trophy
Daniel Alfredsson (1995-96)

Retired Numbers
#8 Frank Finnigan

Captains
Laurie Boschman—1992-93
Brad Shaw/Mark Lamb/
Gord Dineen—1993-94
Randy Cunneyworth—1994-98
Alexei Yashin—1998-99
Daniel Alfredsson—1998-present

Coaches
Rick Bowness—1992-96
Dave Allison—1995-96
Roger Neilson—2001-02 (two games)
Jacques Martin—1995-2004
Bryan Murray—2005-present

All-Star Game Participants
1993 Brad Marsh, Peter Sidorkiewicz
1994 Alexei Yashin
1996 Daniel Alfredsson
1997 Daniel Alfredsson
1998 Daniel Alfredsson, Igor Kravchuk
1999 Ron Tugnutt, Alexei Yashin
2000 Radek Bonk
2001 Radek Bonk, Marian Hossa
2002 Wade Redden
2003 Zdeno Chara, Marian Hossa, Patrick Lalime
2004 Daniel Alfredsson, Marian Hossa, Wade Redden
2007 Dany Heatley

All-Star Team Selections
1998-99
Alexei Yashin (centre, 2nd Team)

2003-04
Zdeno Chara (defence, 1st Team)

2005-06
Daniel Alfredsson (right wing, 2nd Team)
Zdeno Chara (defence, 2nd Team)
Dany Heatley (left wing, 2nd Team)

Jason Spezza celebrates a goal.

Birth of the Stanley Cup

Queen Victoria appointed Sir Frederick Arthur Stanley as the sixth Governor General of Canada on June 11, 1888. The First Baron Stanley of Preston arrived at Government House (Rideau Hall) with four of his ten children (two boys and two girls) and his wife, Constance, and almost immediately every member of the family fell in love with hockey. Isobel, a daughter, played for a Government House ladies team in a game against the Rideau ladies, and the two boys—Arthur and Algernon—also played for a Government House team.

Lord Stanley witnessed his first hockey game in his capacity as Governor General at the Winter Carnival in Montreal in the winter of 1888, the Vics versus the Montreal Amateur Athletic Association (MAAA). The *Montreal Gazette* proudly reported his attendance: "Lord Stanley expressed his great delight with the game of hockey and the expertise of the players."

In early 1892, Ottawa won the OHA championship, and on March 18 a banquet was held in the nation's capital to honour the team. Unable to attend, Lord Stanley prepared an important letter for his aide-de-camp, Lord Kilcoursie, to read to the banqueters. It changed the course of Canadian culture and sporting pursuits (see clipping, left).

Lieutenant Viscount Frederick Rudolph Lambart Kilcoursie, son of the 9th Earl and Baron of Cavan and a part-time playing member of the Rideau Hall Rebels, was given a tremendous cheer upon reading the letter, and the proposals were instantly accepted. Thus, Lord Stanley gave birth not only to the Stanley Cup, but also to the modern schedule, with teams playing an equal number of "home" and "away" games.

Lord Stanley now had to deliver the goods, as it were. He contacted Captain Colville, an aide in London, England, and gave orders to find the finest silversmith in the city to make a small silver bowl. Colville was allowed to expend ten guineas for the commission. He retained a silversmith in Sheffield whose work was retailed by G.H. Collis, Regent Street, London, and using Lord Stanley's coat of arms crafted what was asked of him. The Dominion Challenge trophy, as it was engraved, arrived in Ottawa in early 1893 ready for competition.

Having appointed Sir John Thompson to take over as Governor General when he would return to England in 1893, Lord Stanley now had the responsibility to make one final provision. He appointed two trustees to oversee all matters pertaining to the Cup after his imminent departure: John Sweetland, Ottawa's sheriff, and Philip Ross, a former member of the Rideau Rebels. It was up to these two eximious men to award the Cup each year and to ensure that any worthy opponent in the country had the opportunity to challenge the Cup-winning team for possession of the trophy. Indeed, Lord Stanley set down a thorough constitution by which Sweetland and Ross should govern the Cup:

(1) The winners shall give bond for the return of the cup in good order, when required by the trustees for the purpose of being handed over to any other team that may in turn win;

(2) Each winning team shall have at their own charge, engraved on a silver ring fitted on the cup for that purpose, the name of the team and the year won;

(3) The cup shall remain a challenge cup, and should not become the property of any team, even if won more than once;

(4) In case of any doubt as to the title of any club to claim the position of champions, the cup shall be held or awarded by the trustees as they may think right, their decision being absolute;

(5) Should either trustee resign or otherwise drop out, the remaining trustee shall nominate a substitute.

Terms of victory, however, were still nebulous by the time the AHA season opened at the start of 1893.

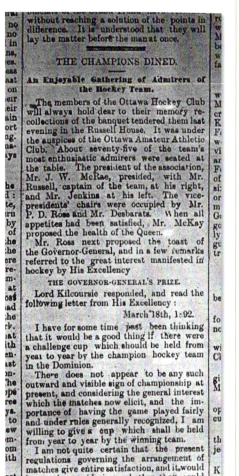

Lord Stanley's only wishes were that the Cup go to "the leading hockey club in Canada," and to this end he believed the AHA to be the most important league in the country. The AHA consisted of five teams: the Ottawa Generals, the Quebec Hockey Club, and three from Montreal—the Victorias, the Crystals, and the MAAA. A 20-game league schedule was drawn up such that each team played eight games, one at home and one away against each opponent, between January 7 and March 17. All games were played outdoors on natural ice, usually on Friday nights, starting at 8:30 p.m.

The finest team in the AHA was the MAAA, champions of the league each year since the AHA formed in 1886. The MAAA was a Montreal social and sporting club that had been established in 1881. It was devoted to the "encouragement of athletic sports, the promotion of physical and mental culture among men, and the providing of rational amusements and recreation for its members." The club promoted three activities in particular—lacrosse, snowshoeing, and bicycling. It became known informally as the "Winged Wheel" because its logo featured a large wheel with wings to encourage the use of the bicycle, a new innovation to North America that same year. (Today, the MAAA is the world's oldest bicycle club.) The MAAA's motto was inscribed in the rim of the wheel: *jungor ut implear*—"I am joined in order that I may be complete." The wings symbolized progress.

The Montreal Hockey Club (MHC) was formed in 1884 and acquired "connected club status" with the MAAA as the club's hockey representatives. Thus, the MAAA hockey club was really the MHC operating under the aegis of the bicycle club (although in order to play for the MHC, one first had to be a member of the MAAA). The Montreal Hockey Club was pioneering for its coherent system of player development. Even though hockey was in its infancy, the MHC had an Intermediate team in 1893. It also inaugurated a junior team the year after to ensure that when members of the MHC team retired or grew too old to play there would be adequately prepared replacements at the ready. Thus, the MHC introduced the farm system to the game.

The Montreal AAA, as the team was officially called, played its home games at the gas-lit Victoria Skating Rink near Dorchester and Stanley streets in downtown Montreal. The smoke congestion in the rink proved to be a constant problem for players and fans alike.

The Ottawa Generals and the MAAA were the class of the 1893 AHA season, and by the end of the schedule only one victory separated the two teams. The MAAA lost only once, to the Generals early in the season, and Ottawa lost twice, once to the Victorias on the first day of the season. The most important game of the year came the night of February 18 when the MAAA beat Ottawa 7-1, and that loss was, in effect, the difference in the standings at the end of the eight-game schedule. Arguably, however, the last game of the year—March 9, 1893—for the MAAA was equally significant because that was the match that confirmed a first-place finish for the team. It was also a victory clouded by controversy.

Officially, Montreal AAA won a close 2-1 victory over cross-town rivals the Crystals at the eponymous Crystal Rink. But what actually happened that night was a different story. The Crystals abandoned their game against Montreal AAA when one of their players, Murray, was given a game misconduct during the second half of a game that ended 2-2 after regulation time. As the teams prepared for overtime, the Crystals assumed they could use Murray now that regulation time had expired. Referee Lewis refused to allow the banished player

Lord Stanley of Preston.

to return, but the Crystals refused to play without him. Lewis awarded the game to Montreal, and so the Stanley Cup was won, indirectly, as a result of this controversial, incomplete game. Had the overtime been played, there is every reason to believe that the MAAA might have lost. The headline the next day in the *Montreal Gazette* said it all: "An Unsatisfactory Game."

As a result of the season's play, trustees Sweetland and Ross named the Montreal AAA winners of the Stanley Cup, believing first place in the AHA entitled the team to be called the best in Canada. And, of course, they welcomed any other league-champion team in the country to challenge the MAAA for the trophy. The Ottawa club was upset with the decision because there had been no playoffs scheduled and because conditions for winning the Cup had not been made clear prior to the start of the season. However, since these matters were left to the discretion of the trustees, the MAAA were named the first winners of the Dominion Challenge trophy.

Excerpted from *Lord Stanley's Cup* by Andrew Podnieks, Fenn Publishing, 2004.

Photo Gallery

Dany Heatley is stopped on the doorstep by J-S Giguere.

Chris Pronger inadvertently tips the puck past J-S Giguere into his own net in game three of the finals.

Daniel Alfredsson celebrates a goal as he brushes goalie Ryan Miller.

Ottawa defenceman Joe Corvo whoops it up after a Senators goal.

Goalie Ray Emery has a worm's-eye view of the play as he smothers the puck

Andy McDonald (out of frame) scored the tying goal in game four of the finals by dekeing Ray Emery and sliding the puck in before Jason Spezza could make the save.